NATURE'S
COLORWAYS

conjuring the chemistry and culture of natural dyes

long thread
M E D I A

Lichens make unlikely colors. They're one of Nature's best-kept secrets. Photo by Joe Coca

Opposite: Fresh indigo leaves produce an ethereal range of blues with little time and effort. Photo by Liz Spencer

contents

Founders
Linda Ligon, Anne Merrow, John P. Bolton
Publisher
John P. Bolton
Director of Marketing
Haydn Strauss

Editorial
Editorial Director
Anne Merrow
Editor
Linda Ligon
Managing Editor
Laura Rintala
Copy Editor
Katie Bright

Creative
Art Director
Kit Kinseth
Production Designer
Mark Dobroth
Production Manager
Trish Faubion

long thread
M E D I A

©Long Thread Media LLC 2021
1300 Riverside Avenue, Suite 206
Fort Collins, Colorado 80524

ISBN
978-1-7350088-2-0 (print)
978-1-7350088-3-7 (digital)

Printed in China by Asia Pacific Offset

Visit us on the web
longthreadmedia.com

LL: Working together to bring *Nature's Colorways* from a morass of ideas and stacks of sticky notes to final publication has been an education for both of us, hasn't it?

I've been captivated by the whole idea of natural dyeing ever since the 1960s, and I thought I knew a lot. I've tried a little bit of everything, produced some beautiful colors, produced a lot of blah beige. The readily available literature back then was skimpy and sometimes misleading (no, common dandelion roots do not produce purple!). But every author I've worked with on this project has taught me useful, even critical, things I didn't know: the rock-bottom basics of indigo chemistry, how to mordant cotton effectively, how to know in an instant whether a lichen will make purple or not.

AM: The most surprising thing I learned over and over is that a lot of what I thought I knew was wrong. You always need two dyestuffs to dye true green? You should always dye last with indigo? All lichens are slow-growing and precious? Tin is a dangerous mordant? All tenets of conventional wisdom turn out not to be true, at least sometimes. Question everything!

LL: And be aware you are not alone. I remember reading about and trying leaf printing directly on fabric back in the early 1970s, and it seemed pretty exotic. Turns out there's a Facebook group just on printing with botanicals that has almost 15,000 followers. And they don't just follow—they do it. There's so much stunning, innovative work. And so much to learn.

AM: That was our gamble, wasn't it—that there would be great interest and resources out there that we could tap into? Every path I've followed, every contact I've made has led to many others. Detours, some of them, but no dead ends. It's been hard to know when to stop.

LL: We could have done a whole book just on indigo. It's had parallel development globally for thousands of years. You've seen it firsthand in the United States and China; I've seen it firsthand in Peru, Central America, Southeast Asia. And seeing how easily you can get beautiful colors from fresh leaves, no complicated processing required, has been a revelation to me. I first saw it in northeastern Laos and thought it was magic. Who knew? Well, lots of people, as it happens. Pulling color out of natural materials is ancient and universal.

AM: When I was in China a few years ago, I was struck by the timelessness of the indigo workshops I visited but also by the precision and efficiency the dyers had mastered. That endless blue thread, going all the way back to the Qin dynasty, or before. My own experiences have been less impressive—my yarn crocked so badly I just threw it out.

LL: Speaking of lack of precision—I'll never forget the time my local weaving guild had a group dye day at my house. One of the pots we worked with was indigo, outdoors on a camp stove. At the end of the day, we dumped the leftover dye into a big puddle in the backyard of our mini-farm, and our white ducks made straight for it. Two-tone ducks!

AM: I've been more of a watcher and collector than a doer. I love that so much natural-dyed fabric is available in the market, from local yarn and fabric shops to International Folk Art Market to high-end fashion boutiques. Knowing the origins of the colors makes the textiles so much more meaningful. And while the old maxim that naturally dyed colors always go together isn't strictly true, I've rarely seen any "ugly" colors. There's commercial potential on a larger scale than we've seen for a couple of centuries. I even have a pair of naturally dyed TOMS shoes.

LL: Most of my natural dyeing has been with plants I've scavenged from here and there. But I'll never forget being in the central plaza in Lima, Peru, and seeing commodity traders with signs saying, "We buy gold and cochineal." Well, the signs were in Spanish, but the meaning was clear: locally harvested cochineal was precious. Even more precious than gold! I think of the Crutchley family story of buying it by the shipload to dye the clothes of the English gentry three hundred years ago. It's pure time travel.

AM: One of the hardest things about creating *Nature's Colorways* has been winnowing down the possibilities. What we've been able to include is only a tiny slice of what's interesting and possible. Like Alice down the rabbit hole, it all gets curiouser and curiouser, and I keep getting curiouser, too.

THE Crutchley Archive

A DYER'S LEGACY

Anita Quye,
Dominique Cardon,
and Jenny Balfour Paul

IN JUNE 2020, the Crutchley Archive collection of eighteenth-century dyers' books gained heritage status when it was inscribed into the United Kingdom Memory of the World Register, part of the UNESCO Memory of the World Programme. The books are rare surviving examples of once commonplace but carefully guarded information from textile dyehouses. They belonged to the Crutchley family, who had a dyeing business on the south bank of the River Thames in London in the early 1700s. For three centuries, the books were passed down the family line, but over time, their importance was forgotten so that they simply became old curiosities. In 2011, the collection was donated to Southwark Council's archive in South London, and in 2014, its significance was finally recognized. This is a personal account of the rediscovery of the Crutchley Archive and the unique insight it gives into the everyday working practices of dyers of eighteenth-century fashion colors. Travel along with us as we discover the richness and depth of these historic documents, analyze their historic colors using modern tools, and explore the neighborhood where eighteenth-century dyers flourished.

Opposite:
Rocque, John, –1762, John Pine, and John Tinney. A plan of the cities of London and Westminster, and borough of Southwark, with the contiguous buildings. London, John Pine & John Tinney, 1746. Map.

Retrieved from the Library of Congress, loc.gov/item/76696823.

Note the location of the Dye House south of Clink Street and east of Dead Man's Place.

EXCEEDING ALL EXPECTATIONS
Anita Quye

The fore-edge and front cover of a Crutchley dye book filled with dyed fabric patterns and dyeing instructions.

Dye book, pre–29 September 1723 to January 1732. Crutchley Archive. SLHLA 2011/5-7. Local History Library and Archive, Southwark Council, London, UK.

ON THE MORNING OF JUNE 20, 2014, when I walked into the John Harvard Library and made my way to the Southwark Local History Library and Archive (SLHLA) at the back, my expectations were modest. I was there to see the Crutchley Archive, a collection of 15 early dyers' books. The seed for examining them was planted three months prior, when I was assessing early eighteenth-century dyers' books for color preservation in The National Archives, Kew. My collaborator there and a curator at the Victoria and Albert Museum both mentioned similarly dated dye books in SLHLA but knew little more about them. My appointment was with Head Archivist Dr. Patricia Dark, who had kindly agreed to my last-minute visit as I headed to a conference in Denmark. A good result would be finding two or three pattern books

with dyeing recipes, I thought, and maybe some dyed samples if I were lucky.

In the reading room, Patricia opened a small archival cardboard box and took out several bundles protected by acid-free tissue. While unwrapping them, she explained that the 15 books had been given as a single private donation, but because of their delicate contents and uncertain meaning, the collection was consigned to storage. The books came from the descendants of John Crutchley, a renowned London dyer who died in 1727. In 2011, the family chose the SLHLA to receive the collection because John owned a dyehouse on Clink Street in Southwark. This was at the edge of today's bustling Borough Market near London Bridge, within a half mile of the John Harvard Library.

The books exceeded all expectations. The large one, roughly 12 by 16 inches with "Pattern Book No 2" written on the hardback cover, was magnificent. Its many pages of neat handwritten dyeing instructions repeated a range of familiar natural dyestuffs—cochineal, madder, brazilwood, logwood, turmeric, archil (orchil lichen), yellow fustic dyewoods, and weld—with the word "graining" in phrases such as "boyle in ye great kettle" (boil in the large cauldron) with "allom" (alum) and "argol" (crude tartar). Cloth types, color shades, people's names, and dates from June 1738 to December 1739 were given. Alongside the texts, stuck to the pages, were neat rows of wool "patterns," samples of dyed fabrics kept for color matching, in shades ranging from deep cherry and zinging scarlet to pale lavender and soft yellows, as fresh and vibrant as if just made. There were two other tomes of similar size and style, also titled "Pattern Book"; the last entry was February 1744.

On the table next to the three tomes lay six smaller books, one coverless, with instructions and patterns. I looked at a foolscap-sized book (about 8½ by 13 inches) with red and violet patterns that had pasted-in inserts of short dyeing instructions written by different people, judging by the handwriting styles, in Flemish or Dutch as well as English. It was in a fragile state with "1726" barely visible on its cover, and it had an SLHLA note beside it that said it was an ingredient book. There were also four softcover books with thin pages, some tinged pink with red splash marks, filled with hundreds of short rough-and-ready lists of dyestuffs, dyeing agents, weights and measures, and occasionally fabric types, plus hand-drawn mono-

Alongside the texts . . . were neat rows of wool "patterns," samples of dyed fabrics kept for color matching, in shades ranging from deep cherry and zinging scarlet to pale lavender and soft yellows, as fresh and vibrant as if just made.

grams similar to weavers' marks that I had seen in historical tapestry borders. Last were two books stiffly bound in leather, with names and cash amounts from a few pounds sterling to thousands in entries dated 1721 to 1725.

I was astounded. This was unlike anything I had seen or even heard of. I suspected some might be of national, or even international, historical interest. Certainly, the beautiful three-hundred-year-old colors would be enormously intriguing for anyone interested in textile history, and dyers would be fascinated by the dyeing instructions. The Crutchley Archive was potentially very precious.

As thrilling as this sounds, the implications for a resource-stretched local-authority library were huge. The time and skill of staff for even bringing the collection out of storage for study, and the expense, special knowledge, and logistics of preservation and exhibition would have to be considered. What this meant for the Crutchley Archive would depend on how important it turned out to be, but already I saw risks for the dye colors. The radiant and subtle shades of the dye samples could be lost even under the most careful protective lighting in archives and museums.

Patricia accepted my offer to research the collection's contents to understand its historical significance and make recommendations for color preservation. I promised a return visit and written assessment. At the conference in Denmark I met my long-time colleague Dr. Dominique Cardon. The timing was perfect for comparison with her research on French dyers' archives of a similar date. Our excitement at what the archive promised was more than enough encouragement to plan a collaboration. I also approached Dr. Jenny Balfour Paul, who was equally intrigued and delighted to be involved.

I returned to SLHLA in late August for a closer examination of the collection with Dr. Gwen Fereday, dyer and color-matching specialist at the University of Middlesex, and a longer discussion with Patricia and archivist Lisa Moss about access and permission to initiate research with Dominique and Jenny. I received funding from the Textile Conservation Foundation and Worshipful Company of Dyers (WCD) for two week-long study visits to SLHLA so that the three of us could pool our skills; the funding also enabled me to employ Dr. Jing Han to assist with dye analysis and lightfastness trials.

Our research team met at SLHLA in June and November 2016 and set about discovering the dyers' choices of materials and methods to understand what the Crutchley business produced. We each knew what to look for and had particular points of interest. Dominique evaluated the color shades and creation, red dyes, and cloth types; Jenny explored the dyehouse location and what this meant for the Crutchleys in eighteenth-century London as well as the use of indigo in dyehouses; and I compared the dyes in the patterns against those written in the instructions.

Our task was to examine each book and photograph every page possible so our visual and text analyses could continue after the study trips. Even with the work divided among us, it took a great deal of time, partly because of the care needed to open the books and handle the delicate pages—some weakened from years of damp and mold and the weight of the attached patterns—but mostly because of the remarkable details we saw for the first time. The handwriting was legible, and spelling variations and shorthand for the materials were understandable, but it was an enormous amount of information to take in from more than a thousand technical dyeing instructions and a similar number of patterns.

We enlisted the help of Ian Mackintosh, archivist for the WCD, to search for livery and professional status information about John Crutchley and his sons. Lisa arranged a meeting for us with Annie Crutchley, who acquainted us with the family's history and allowed Jenny access to private documents, including wills.

Description of dyeings done in June 1741. Three are for Mr. Jonathan Collier: Number 395 describes the processes to dye 15 long ells scarlet on a scarlet flat (reuse of a dye or "graining" bath for scarlet) with madder and cochineal; number 396 describes dyeing 15 long ells rose on a pink flat with good and damaged cochineal; Number 398, bottom, describes dyeing one long cloth "visne" (wine color) with logwood, madder, and cochineal, reusing a scarlet dyebath for a bay. Number 397 describes dyeing one hair list drab (the highest quality of broadcloth) rose on a pink flat with good cochineal and nuancing it with warm water and piss for Mr. Dingley.

Pattern Book 3, January 1739/40 to February 1744. Crutchley Archive. Local History Library and Archive, Southwark Council, London, UK.

Descriptions of dyeings done in November 1740. The three top entries are for Mr. Monk; they describe the processes to dye two long bays in fresh baths with different proportions of young fustic, turmeric, and crop madder. The resulting colors are not identified by name. Numbers 347 and 348 are for Mr. Wenham; they are processes for three long bays dyed first with young fustic and turmeric in reused madder dyebaths and then top-dyed with madder in a reused madder dyebath for red. The bottom samples describe the processes to dye four cloths scarlet with cochineal and a little madder, after a mordant bath with young fustic and a little cochineal added.

Pattern Book 3, January 1739/40 to February 1744. Crutchley Archive. Local History Library and Archive, Southwark Council, London, UK.

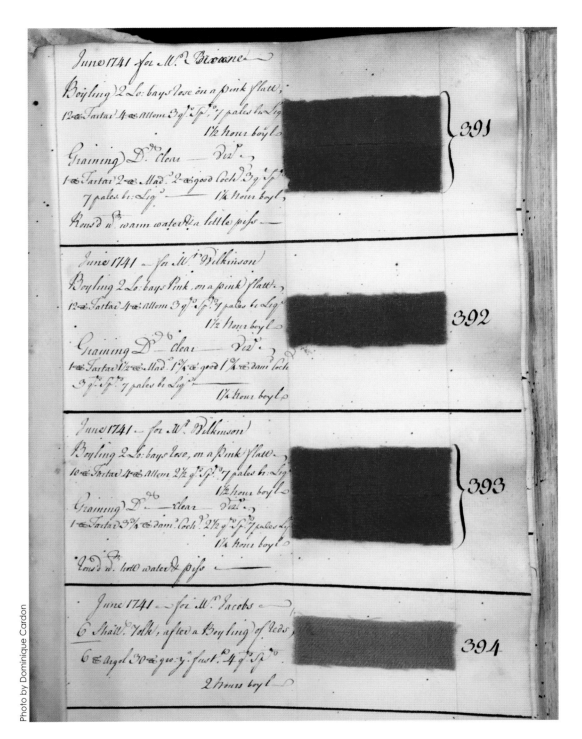

Description of dyeings done in June 1741: Number 391, for Mr. Browne, two long bays rose with cochineal and madder in a reused dyebath for pinks; numbers 392 and 393 for Mr. Wilkinson, two long bays pink and two long bays rose in reused dyebaths for pinks; number 394, for Mr. Jacobs, six shalloons yolk color with young fustic in a reused mordant bath for madder reds.

Pattern Book 3, January 1739/40 to February 1744. Crutchley Archive. Local History Library and Archive, Southwark Council, London, UK.

Dr. David Mitchell, who had looked at the dye books before 2011 for research on London dyers, shared a family tree and information he had found about another Crutchley dyehouse in "The Maese," the area around today's Great Maze Pond in Southwark. I asked Gary Bankhead, a research fellow in underwater archaeology conservation at Durham University, to look at the monograms in the book, and he saw similarities to marks on medieval lead cloth seals. He recommended research to compare them to historical cloth seals recovered from the Thames riverside at Southwark and now in the Museum of London and the British Museum. Jenny also found similarities between the Crutchley monograms and bale marks in the mid-eighteenth-century Passavant's Exeter Cloth Dispatch Book. Many others offered assistance and wished to see the books, but we needed to focus on the initial research into this fantastic resource and its scope, so instead we shared as much as we could at conferences.

Some discoveries we recognized quickly, while others took time to percolate. "Graining" was evidently core to the Crutchleys' business, mentioned from the first to the last dyeing instruction. Dominique understood the Crutchley "in grain" method to be equivalent to contemporary French dyeing regulations for colorfast dyeing. The Crutchley dyers used mostly colorfast but costly red colorants, such as cochineal and madder, with some nuances obtained by adding noncolorfast dyewoods such as brazilwood and logwood for crimsons and "wine" colors, or fustic and turmeric in the mordant-

ing for scarlets. "Out of grain" meant the less colorfast mode of dyeing, involving brazilwood, logwood, and orchil in a "clear flatt" (fresh dyebath), or recycling a mordant or scarlet dyebath to "rouse" the final desired shade or to imitate "in grain" colors. Recycled mordant baths were also used for "buff" yellows. These fresh and recycled "flatts" enabled the dyers to achieve desirable and exquisite shadings. The patterns for each client in the two large books dated 1738 to 1744 were especially interesting, showing the subtle hues that could be created from different flatts, dyestuffs, and dyeing agents.

The dyers distinguished different grades of madder and cochineal and made good use of the lower-quality cochineal damaged by seawater as ships' cargo. "Spirits" was another frequent word in the instructions, meaning a tin mordant prepared with nitric acid, tin metal, and salt that enabled the creation of vibrant scarlet shades not possible with alum alone. The Crutchleys outsourced indigo dyeing to another dyehouse, indicated by the instruction "to be wadded . . . at London," probably on the north bank of the Thames near the WCD. Jenny found a bill for "wadding" at £2 2s as proof of this practice.

As it turned out, the dye books were older than 1726, with pages dated 1722 and inserts going back to 1716. All the pre-1728 dye books were highly descriptive. Detailed instructions recommended sizes of dyeing kettles and when to use water from a spring or from the tidal estuary of the "River Tham[e]s," presumably based on mineral and salt content differences. The 1726 book that SLHLA had noted as an ingredient

Photo by Dominique Cardon

Dyeing instructions in Flemish or Old Dutch and in English from several dyers to dye "Salsberey" broadcloth and long cloth in scarlet color with cochineal and best-grade madder with mordants of alum and tin "spirits."

The "In Grain Book," 1726, inserts 1716–1728. Crutchley Archive. Local History Library and Archive, Southwark Council, London, UK.

book turned out to be the "In Grain Book," elevating its importance, although it was too fragile for us to examine beyond the first few pages. The most astonishing discovery was that the Flemish or Old Dutch instructions had been translated by English-speaking dyers, and they had replicated sets of patterns. Before and during the eighteenth century, dyers from Netherlandic countries had a worldwide reputation for skill with madder and cochineal dyes, and this was the first evidence we knew of for this knowledge diffusion. The information in the books pointed to the work of master dyers and must have been highly protected by the Crutchley family.

Dominique determined that the Crutchleys' business was mostly concerned with two types of wool textiles. The majority were worsteds and lightweight woolens, including mainly shalloons (twills), bays (mixed woolen- and worsted-spun yarns), and an interesting range of high-quality broadcloths, or hard-wearing, densely woven fulled and shorn fabrics from various textile centers in the south and west of England.

In cash books dated 1721 to 1725, Jenny found 147 individual names, including a woman and the merchant tailor Caleb Flower, who was married to John's daughter, Anne, plus references to the East India Company and South Sea Company. If these are orders, the financial transactions ranged from 5 shillings to nearly £2,500 sterling, which is equivalent to approximately £50 to £250,000, or US $70 to more than $350,000 today.

Dominique brought a portable spectrophotometer to measure the colors of the patterns in the books and make comparisons to those of the French dyers she was researching. To identify the dyes in the patterns, I needed to remove threads no longer than 10 millimeters for chemical analysis in Glasgow. The SLHLA allowed this, and once we understood the books well enough to know what was most pertinent for our research and color preservation, I settled on 36 patterns. Dye analysis revealed that light-sensitive dyes were still in the patterns, making control of lighting levels and exposure times critical for studying and displaying the dye books. Jing and I discovered that the dyestuffs in the instructions closely matched the dyes in the patterns for the books dated 1738 to 1744. In the oldest book, we often found cochineal and madder in patterns when the instructions said brazilwood and cochineal, and woad/indigo where they said logwood. It is not clear why, but less colorfast dyes have faded,

or mistakes may have been made when inserting patterns next to instructions.

Once we knew the books' contents better and their 1716 to 1744 timeline, their meaning fell into place with the Crutchleys' business papers and wills. Key dates were the start of John's business by 1718; the marriage in 1721 of John's daughter, Anne, to Caleb Flower; the increase of the ownership share in the Clink Street dyehouse for one of John's sons in 1722; John's will of 1723 mentioning the Maese dyehouses and Clink Street; and in 1727, the deaths of John and another son who was a dyer. The five earliest dye books and the two cash books spanned this period of significant family change. The last entry was just before the death of another son, Coleman, in 1744.

So complex and rich is the Crutchley Archive that it took three years to fully process our initial findings and understand them well enough to publish in the journal *Textile History* in 2020. Taking this time to think about what we found benefited the strong case to nominate the Crutchley Archive for the Memory of the World Register. The research has also helped SLHLA secure a grant to conserve the most fragile books, including the "In Grain Book."

Although our funding ended in 2016, the research team and SLHLA have maintained contact to discuss and apply the research, and we have involved each other in talks, conferences, publications, and plans for further research funding. Our enthusiasm and appreciation for these very special books grows stronger—even though the protected status means it is unlikely that we will be able to get so close to the books again.

The natural dyes used by the Crutchley dyers have stimulated interest for community gardens in Southwark to grow dye plants for local workshops and other educational ideas, and the glorious pattern colors have inspired architects with the color scheme for Southwark Council's new Walworth Heritage Center, where the Crutchley books will be featured. This all resonates personally for me, having spent my early childhood in the east end of London, and I am pleased to have played a part in uncovering this rich textile history. As our research continues, it is certain to bring more surprises about textile dyeing history and boundless joy through its beautiful colors.

EXPLORING THE CRUTCHLEYS' COLORS
Dominique Cardon

OF THE 15 BOOKS in the Crutchley Archive, nine relate specifically to the processes involved in dyeing. While one of them only gives recipes, the eight others belong to the small group of historical documents that provide clues for understanding historical colors. They give precise descriptions of the colorants and processes used to obtain a particular hue, identified by its color name, but what makes them invaluable is that they provide a corresponding sample of dyed fabric.

Even excluding those parts of the books in poor state of preservation that make the samples inaccessible or discolored, the Crutchley dye books offer an amazing corpus of 775 dyed samples whose colors look well preserved, are defined by color names, and correspond to a precise description of the whole process by which they have been obtained.

The prospects this opens for research and dye experiments have two limitations, however. Since the Crutchleys specialized in mordant dyeing with red dyestuffs, the entries overwhelmingly represent the section of the color spectrum ranging from orange to red to purple, with lighter shades obtained by recycling the mordant and dyebaths of the expensive saturated hues most favored by the Crutchleys' clients. The most common color is scarlet, also mentioned by its names in Flemish or Dutch, which represents 37.8 percent of the number of samples described by a color name. Next come crimson, then buff, pink, the "wine" colors, flesh, red, rose, violet, cherry, aurora, blossom, orange, purple, yolk, gold, yellow, and silver,

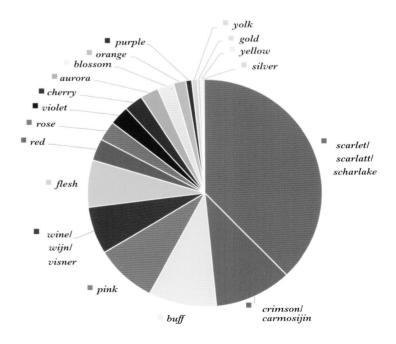

in rapidly descending order of frequency. The Crutchleys' palette is therefore described with 18 color names, enriched when needed by adjectives corresponding to various degrees of lightness ("light cherry"), saturation ("full flesh"), and hue ("scarlet aurora"), as is done today by colorists.

The second limitation is that entries specify the type of textile and the number of pieces being dyed, but they almost never provide the corresponding weight of fabric, which would allow calculations for proportions of ingredients in relation to the material to be dyed. A typical entry reads as follows: "2 longe bocking bays pinks boild in spring watter with 13 pd of alum, 10 pd & a ½ of argel & 1 mog of spirits; graind upon a fresh flat with 4 pd of mader & 1 pd and ½ of argel & 2 pd & ¾ & 2 ounces of cochenel. Boil as long as cloths." (Bottom note): "Use archill in ye graining, 12 spoonfulls." Extensive research is still needed to collect reliable data on the piece weights of the many types of wool fabrics mentioned.

Fortunately, the colorimetric study that we conducted on the samples offers new possibilities for partly overcoming this difficulty and allowing precise and objective comparisons to be made with the colors of other dyed samples, either figuring in other historical dye books or resulting from experiments to reproduce the processes described in the Crutchley books at different scales. For this purpose, colorimetric measurements of all the samples whose state of preservation allowed were performed with a spectrophotometer. The results are expressed in the most widely used international system of specification for surface colors and particularly for colors of textiles: the CIELAB (L*a*b*) chromatic space proposed in 1976 by the Commission Internationale de l'Eclairage (International Commission on Illumination). Specification of the color of each sample is also expressed in the complementary CIE L*C*h* system. In this chromatic space, color is defined by three coordinates:

- L* indicates lightness on the axis of grays (from black, corresponding to L* = 0, to white, corresponding to L* = 100).
- On the a* axis, green (negative values of a*) is opposed to red (positive values of a*).
- Along the b* axis, blue (negative values of b*) is opposed to yellow (positive values of b*).

These data allow calculation of chromaticity (C*) and hue angle (h°):
- C* describes the chroma or saturation based on a given level on the axis of grays (C* = 0 meaning no saturation; C* = 100 meaning maximum saturation).
- h° defines hue in a circular way (0° = magenta red; 90° = yellow; 180° = green; 270° = blue; 359° = nearly magenta red).

Because they are precisely located within this

Description of the mordanting and dyeing process used to dye two pieces of long bocking bays into pink some time after June 1728, and corresponding sample.

Crutchley Archive. Local History Library and Archive, Southwark Council, London, UK.

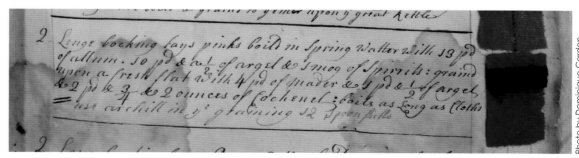

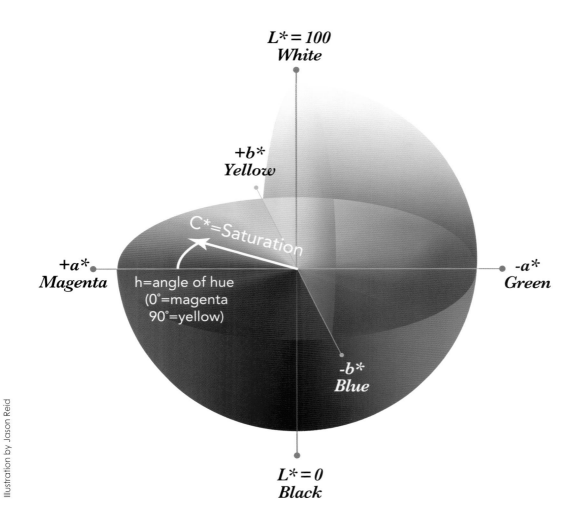

L*= 100
White

+b*
Yellow

C*=Saturation

+a*
Magenta

h=angle of hue
(0°=magenta
90°=yellow)

-a*
Green

-b*
Blue

L*= 0
Black

The CIE L*a*b*
chromatic
space.

chromatic space, the colors of the samples in the Crutchleys' dye books can now be used as references for all kinds of experiments to reproduce their colors or to make comparisons with the color gamuts of other dyers from different periods of history or different parts of the world; their chromatic specifications just need to be compared with those of dyed samples measured and characterized by the same method. In this way, it has recently been possible to demonstrate that some madder reds dyed at the Crutchleys' dyehouses were almost identical with the madder reds of several contemporary

dyers in the south of France.

This work represents a new step in research that I am currently pursuing to collect a data bank of the chromatic characteristics of as many dyed textile samples preserved in historical documents as possible. This will provide a sound basis on which to follow the evolutions of color names, map the chromatic spaces to which the different names correspond, and try to relate such information on color terminology and chromatic content with the evolution of dyeing technologies during the era of presynthetic dyes.

A view of the River Thames looking east toward Southwark Bridge, which opened in 1921. This photo was taken on the south bank of the river, at a spot very near Clink Street where a Crutchley dyehouse once stood. Famous City of London landmarks, such as the dome of St. Paul's Cathedral, can be seen on the north side, as well as relatively modern wood posts along the riverbank.

A PLACE IN TIME
Jenny Balfour Paul

CAYENNE, VANILLA, AND SESAME Courts; Cardamom Building; Java and Jamaica Wharves; India House. What's in a name? Stroll around the docks of London's Southwark Borough on the south bank of the Thames and the names of today's hipster flats and offices in converted warehouses summon an exotic age. Some residents claim to catch whiffs of cinnamon in the streets, spreading from cracks of the past. When the Crutchley dyers were at work, their dyes were unloaded here from the holds of merchant ships alongside spices and "drugs." They were stored in these warehouses in jute, calico, and leather sacks and bales or in wooden cases and were haggled over as they changed hands.

In the seventeenth century, an increasingly consumerist society in Europe drove demand for quality textiles with a greater color range. The demand could be met until the nineteenth century, largely due to the dominance of colonialism, which ensured a vast supply of foreign dyestuffs to Europe's ports from East and West. The mercantile British Empire, centered on London, enabled the Crutchley dyers to color cloth with an astonishing range of hues.

In the eighteenth century, the Thames was one of the world's busiest waterways, with docks expanding rapidly along its shores. The Pool of London in particular, where the river is deep east of London Bridge, provided ideal anchorage for tall-masted vessels. Today's ships pass sedately along the river, but when the Crutchleys were at work, it was very different. The river was so congested that it could be crossed from deck to deck. Small boats ferried goods to numerous piers accessed by stone steps. Sitting on the kempt promenade today, within a stone's throw of the former Crutchley dyeworks off Clink Street, I imagine the scene three centuries ago at this point where river meets sea. Stumps of former jetties emerge from the shoreline mud when the tide drops, reminders of the past's exuberant, harsh, and fetid reality.

John Rocque's famous *Map of London* of 1747, with a scale of 26 inches to a mile, shows Vinegar Yard, Pepper Alley, Pickle Herring Stairs, brewhouses, Tanner Street, and the dyehouses themselves. Here again names tell their tale, peopled with all who worked, drank, ate, and slept here: brewers, sailors, tanners, actors, prostitutes, undertakers, merchants, and tradespeople of all kinds including immigrants from overseas, some of whom joined the communities of dyers. Dirty Lane and Foul Lane also feature on the map: imagine a time of no sewerage or proper garbage disposal. Could people

today even tolerate the mixed smells from animal and human excrement, rotting fish, leather tanning, and cloth and dyeing processes that included "sigg/piss," which was stale urine (ammonia) by the bucketful, an essential free ingredient if you can hold your nose. It's hard to imagine how insalubrious the inner streams, waterways, and docks, as well as the Thames herself, must have been at that time. No wonder the residences of the wealthy were built well west of Southwark, safely upwind.

By boat along the tideline and by handcart beside the wharves and alleys came the packages of dyestuffs, smelling of long voyages, of the other spices they were stored with (some, such as turmeric, doubling as dye and medicine), and of their places of origin. Madder root came from Europe, but dyes for the brightest red cloths had farther to travel. Millions of tiny cochineal insects were harvested from prickly pears by coerced indigenous labor in Central America and Peru and were shipped in huge quantities to Spain for onward export. These cargoes were second in value only to gold and silver, well worth the risks of shipwreck or pirate attack. A valuable Spanish galleon, the *Concepcion*, sank off Hispaniola (now the Dominican Republic) in a storm in 1641 with a cargo that included

A "Short Worcester or Salisbury" broadcloth dyed in May 1741. The two patterns of number 384 show a "violet" color with madder, damaged cochineal, and alum on a blue "wadded" (woad/indigo-dyed) ground.

Pattern Book 3, January 1739/40 to February 1744. Crutchley Archive. Local History Library and Archive, Southwark Council, London, UK.

Photo by Jenny Balfour Paul

1,200 chests and bags of cochineal and indigo. Some of the indigo was recovered in 1978 and proved potent despite centuries on the seabed. The *Albemarle,* an East Indiaman on her maiden voyage, carrying indigo from southern India along with a precious cargo of diamonds, coffee, silks, and pepper, was wrecked in 1708 soon after entering the English Channel on the homestretch to London after three years at sea. The wreck was never recovered, but contemporary reports claim the seas were stained blue from indigo for many weeks.

Had this indigo reached London, it would have been stored on the north bank of the Thames opposite Southwark. The nineteenth-century *Dickens's Dictionary of Trades* describes vast "Blue Warehouses" of the East India Company in Fenchurch and Jewry Streets in the city of London. In the Crutchleys' time, the insoluble stonelike cakes of penetrating indigo dye pigment, releasing blue dust that got everywhere, were made in the age-old Indian way: Indigo leaves were soaked in large tanks of water (to create colorless indoxyl), then the leaves were removed and oxygen was added by vigorous beating until a bright blue foam appeared. Indigo pigment subsequently precipitated into a claylike paste that dried into a durable, easily traded commodity. This system was emulated and refined in the European colonies of the Caribbean and in Central America and the southern United States using slave labor.

Dyeing with indigo required specialized knowledge, and the Crutchleys outsourced their woad/indigo dyeing; their pattern books note that fabric was first "wadded" (i.e., woaded) at London and then "topped" in-house to create various shades such as "violatts." (Wadding refers to the hybrid vat, started with woad and reinforced with an addition of indigo pigment.) "At London" meant across the river in the city. Picture horses crossing London Bridge pulling carts piled high with undyed cloth, or small boats low in the water with the weight of heavy bales of cloth, and then the return to the Crutchley dyehouses with cloth now dyed all shades of blue and ready for overdyeing. Such was the lure of color in all its subtleties.

Heavy logs of dyewood provided "lesser" dyes and doubled as ships' ballast. From Central America and the Caribbean came logwood for blues and blacks and brazilwood for red, a color also obtained from sanderswood or red sandalwood that decimated the forests on India's coast of Coromandel. The *Svecia,* a Swedish East Indiaman contemporary with the Crutchleys, was wrecked off the Scottish island of Ronaldsay. When it was found in 1975 by a team led by underwater explorer Rex Cowan, many billets of dyewood were discovered. Islanders still dye local sheep's wool with this wood when it washes ashore.

Those who could afford clothing skillfully dyed in Crutchley's and other dyehouses probably gave little thought to the sources of the dyes, the labor involved, and the effect on the environment. Such is the continued craving for color and new hues to suit fashions and trends that we largely turn a blind eye today both to exploitation of workers and to the pollution of rivers and oceans from hidden factories and container shipping that form today's chain of supply.

A page of "Short Worcester or Salisbury" broadcloths and long cloth dyed in May 1741.

Pattern Book 3, January 1739/40 to February 1744. Crutchley Archive. Local History Library and Archive, Southwark Council, London, UK.

The mighty Thames has a history from Neolithic times and saw an exceptional flourish of activity in the eighteenth century. What's in its name? For merchant seamen, the Thames has long been known simply as "London River."

THE SIMPLE MAGIC OF
fresh indigo

John Marshall

WHO WOULDN'T BE ENTHRALLED while watching the magic of alchemy as juice from the leaves of the earth is transformed before our very eyes into the boundless blues of the sky overhead? Since ancient times, this process has been enshrouded in mystery, its secret science carefully guarded and handed down only to trusted stewards. As a result, many creative but misguided concepts encrust the historical recipes available to us.

Let me chip away some of that crust and expose the clean and logical beauty of this process for what it is—one of the simple pleasures of nature.

To begin with, let's take a look at the leaf. As with all plants, it is made up of a collection of cells, and each part of each cell has its own role to play. There is really only one portion that we

are interested in at the moment—the element that will later give us blue. It's called *indican*, but what's in a name? Let's decide to call it *pre-blue* for the purposes of this article. To make our blue, we need to add one more ingredient, and that is simply the oxygen in the air we breathe.

The pre-blue is trapped within the leaf. As long as it is encased, it does us no good. If we somehow break through this barrier, we can release it. Released, we can partner it with oxygen, and their union will produce blue. If we interrupt this union, the blue will revert to its components, pre-blue and oxygen. We may convert the elements back and forth between these two states to suit our needs. That is really all that there is to the theory of working with indigo. Art, science, and experience help us to know when and how to manipulate these states.

Amount of leaves to
cloth, number of dips,
time, temperature—
these are just a few of
the variables that affect
the hue of silk fabrics
dyed with fresh indigo.

Photo by Joe Coca

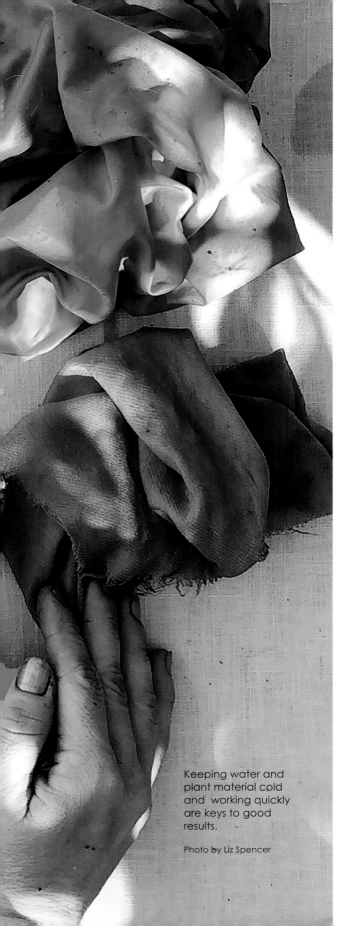

Keeping water and plant material cold and working quickly are keys to good results.

Photo by Liz Spencer

pre-blue + oxygen = blue

blue − oxygen = pre-blue

Let's first visit removing the pre-blue from the leaf. One way to approach it is simply through brute force.

Select a few large, well-shaped indigo leaves from your garden or those well-tended pots on your sunny deck. Rinse them with cold water and blot dry. Take a piece of silk cloth—this may be just a scrap or a beautiful, rolled-edge scarf—and spread it flat on a firm, smooth surface, such as a tabletop or linoleum floor. Lay one or more leaves out in a pleasing arrangement on the silk. Spread a sheet of clear plastic—a 1-gallon-size baggie will work well—over the composition. Now have at it with a rounded rock, mallet, or cowboy boot! That's it! Really let out all your frustrations.

Simply pounding fresh leaves (in this case, on Japanese wool crêpe) releases the pre-blue pigment and exposes it to oxygen, making a permanent print.

Photo by Joe Coca

one set of leaves and wash it right away to achieve blue imagery; and then go back with a fresh application of leaves which you allow to dry before rinsing. This will give you a beautifully nuanced range of blues and greens.

Now that you've had your first taste, are you feeling like expanding your operation? We're going to gather up a whole bunch of leaves this time, early in the morning while everyone else is sleeping. You may take time to individually select leaves as you pick them from the stems, or you may simply gather stems and all and sort them out later.

Separate the leaves from the stems if you haven't already done so. Place a handful of leaves in a blender and fill with cold water. Blend on medium or high until everything is nicely sliced, diced, and pulverized. About a minute or so should do it. This will break up the cell walls and allow the pre-blue to be released into the water where you can access it.

Strain the slurry through a colander with a handkerchief lining—this will separate out the vegetable matter, which may be tossed back into the garden or compost. The remaining juice will be our dyebath. During its time in the blender, the pre-blue was introduced to the oxygen. Keep the liquid cool.

Gently slip a prewashed silk scarf, necktie, or whatever you like into the mix and gently swish it from time to time. This will ensure even coverage. (I'm suggesting silk because that's the best fiber for this process. Cotton or other cellulose fibers just won't work very well.)   The

The goal here is to separate the pre-blue from the cells of the leaf. Take care not to damage the silk in the process. As the pre-blue is exposed, it will combine with oxygen, and after a short wait, turn blue. At this point, two paths are open to you. You may wash the fabric now in cold water before the leaf-juice dries and you'll be left with a clean robin's-egg blue ▢ . Or allow it to dry before rinsing, and you'll have a nice blue and teal-green print ▢ . It's your call.

If you're feeling unfulfilled, you may print with

Photo by Liz Spencer

Fresh-leaf indigo
samples drying
on the author's
outdoor deck.

Photo by Liz Spencer

A range of blues and greens on raw silk are produced as the dyebath exhausts.

longer you leave the silk to soak, the deeper the color will develop into a rich blue. If you wash your dyed silk before allowing it to dry, you will be rewarded with a bluer blue. This may be anywhere from a robin's-egg blue ▯ to a rich peacock blue ▮. If you let it dry before rinsing, as before, you'll be able to retain a range of teal blues and greens.

There are other ways to break down the cell structure to release the pre-blue. For example, salt may be pressed into service. The salt crystals will shred the cell walls and at the same time draw out the moisture and the pre-blue along with it.

Gather up a handful of the plucked leaves and toss them into a large bowl. Sprinkle liberally with table salt. Get in there with your hands and squeeze and mash and pulverize. Add your silk. In the midst of this activity, oxygen will be introduced. Without gloves, your hands will become quite stained—but where's the fun in wearing gloves? Welcome to the tribe of the Blue Handed—wear the color with pride!

Wait until it dries and it will retain a distinctive green cast As the salt softens and dissolves, it forces the water in the leaves out (and indican with it) in an attempt to dilute the saline con-

The freshness and health of the leaves affect the resulting color. The top fabric was dyed with leaves that were past their prime.

Photo by Liz Spencer

Ethereal blues can be coaxed from fresh leaves of Japanese indigo.

Photo by Joe Coca

centrate. It's the same thing that happens when you sprinkle salt on shredded cabbage to make a wilted salad. This is why we don't have to add water to this step; the leaf itself supplies the liquid needed with the help of the salt to make it accessible. The longer you knead the mashed-up mix, the darker the color will become. Rinse the silk before it dries and, yes, you get a bluer blue.

I've shared three strategies for direct application. However, there are many other approaches, including all the time-honored ways of extraction and fermentation that have been practiced around the globe for centuries. Just keep in mind

that any and all plans to attain blue involve combining or separating pre-blue and oxygen— nothing more complicated than that.

With a sense of adventure and permitting your- self to learn as you go, you'll be able to get along just fine working with indigo. It has only the very simplest of needs. Pre-blue needs oxygen to turn blue. The ultimate truth in the universe.

Additional reading: *Singing the Blues: Soulful Dyeing for All Eternity, with John Marshall as Your Guide.* (See Resources, page 109.)

GROW YOUR OWN

As long as you have at least a sunny balcony and some healthy dirt, you'll be able to grow Japanese indigo (*Persicaria tinctoria*). It grows well in most subtropical and temperate climates—even as far north as Greenland with proper care. It is not drought tolerant, but it is otherwise very easy to grow. If you can grow basil where you live, you'll be able to grow *Persicaria tinctoria*.

The seeds may be purchased from many sources online. I like to recommend seed from Rowland Ricketts: rickettsindigo.com. To get the seeds started, plant them in shallow trays filled with rich potting soil early in the spring. A very sunny window or greenhouse will give you the hardiest starts. Don't plant outside until all danger of frost has passed. For me, here in northern California, that is normally the first of June.

Transfer the seedlings to their new location. Full sun is preferred, but they will grow well with some shade. The young roots will be tangled, but gently tearing them apart will do no harm. Space the clumps of four or five seedlings about a foot or two apart.

Summer is the rainy season in Japan, so keep your plants moist and water daily whenever possible. Good drainage is required, but never let the roots dry out completely.

The plants will be ready to use for dyeing once they are 2 to 3 feet tall, about midsummer. For fresh-leaf pounding or dyeing as I've described here, you can strip leaves from the stems; they will soon sprout new ones. Or you may cut the stalks down to about 6 to 12 inches from the base; they will quickly recover with a new crop of fresh growth.

Photo by Liz Spencer

botanical printing

ART ADVENTURES WITH PLANT PIGMENTS

Wendy Feldberg

MAKING ART WITH THE COLORS inherent in plants is my creative adventure. I am a lifelong gardener; for me, natural color is a living creation in the landscape and in the plants I tend and forage. As a fiber artist with a mighty stash of papers, vintage textiles, and plants, I am inevitably drawn to natural dyeing, particularly its applications to direct printing with plant dyes.

BOTANICAL PRINTING AS ART

Commonly known as ecoprinting, botanical printing is a contemporary fiber art genre that extracts color and pattern from plants, transferring these onto textiles and paper by placing plant and textile or paper in direct contact with each other, then typically steaming, simmering, or cold soaking them together as bundles or stacks.

Terms such as bundle dyeing, compression printing, contact printing, direct printing, ecodyeing, leaf printing, plant pounding, plant printing, and several others can all refer to the ecoprinting process. This proliferation of interchangeable terms reflects an international growth of interest in ecoprinting, explored as art by India Flint in her influential book *Eco Colour: Botanical Dyes for Beautiful Textiles* and eagerly investigated by many fiber artists.

Making a basic ecoprint is straightforward. Premordanted with alum to fix color, papers or textiles are bundled tightly with plants, then steamed or simmered in hot water. Other methods also yield ecoprints: cold soaking, solar dyeing, microwaving, composting for months, or "compression" printing using equipment such as a hammer, steam iron, pasta maker, etching press, or heat press. Each of these processes extracts pigments from the plants and affixes them to mordanted paper or cloth, not always as the

uniform color aimed for in a traditional dyepot but often in prints that the artist can freely manipulate before or after printing. Rusted metals, liquid dyes, and powdered plant and mineral extracts may be processed along with the plants for added surface complexity; colors can be shifted in the bundle or after opening it with natural-dye modifiers such as iron, soda ash, and vinegar.

The result is extraordinary patterning unique to each printing session—often in otherwise hidden colors. Sometimes the print reproduces plants and colors so realistically as to show even the tiny veins on a leaf; other times, it reveals abstract forms and impressionistic color washes from dye migrations or even surprise colors provoked by the process. Whatever the goal, a key principle for obtaining a satisfying print is to place plants in very close contact with a mordanted paper or textile substrate to make a "bundle." Artists can choose to aim for spontaneous dye mixing for abstracted color effects, or they can manage

Far left: Lay out plants over about half the cloth or paper. Here, maple, sumac, coreopsis, and sand cherry.

Left: It is safe to use copper pipe in the bundles.

Opposite page: Summer blooms captured on paper.

color mixing by distributing fewer plants over less than half of the substrate. One technique found to create a clear print—that is, one with crisply defined shapes—is to place a barrier such as parchment paper over the plants so that the dye transfers onto only one surface.

When plant-substrate bundles are heat-processed, they are best enclosed between covers (such as cardboard, ceramic, or metal) or coiled tightly around wooden or copper rods; this ensures direct contact between plant and substrate. String, fabric strips, and/or binder clips fastened around the bundles create strong pressure and close contact. Appropriate mordants for fixing color on cellulose and protein fibers, choice of substrates, longer or shorter processing times, water quality, plant part, and plant season all play important roles in ensuring a happy print outcome.

PLANTS FOR BOTANICAL PRINTING

Plants for ecoprints can be garden-grown, store-bought, field- or fridge-foraged, fresh, dried, or frozen. Most of the plants listed on page 38 are native to my region (USDA Zone 4); your own region is sure to offer color-giving plants that are safe to use. Some plants or plant parts print their colors as seen in nature or in a traditional dyepot, while others deliver seasonal or process-induced surprises. Tannin-rich plants such as sumac and oak may influence nearby plants in the ecoprint bundle by contributing to colorfastness or color change.

Colorplay for Botanical Printing

If you are curious about how to enhance colors or rescue wimpy prints, the simplest strategy is to print the work again! But in the spirit of "What if?" and by using a few common kitchen chemicals, rusty nails, a natural dyebath, or natural media for art, you can take your colors and prints even further with these playful ideas.

1. Using pH modifiers

Intentional color mixing with natural dyes in ecoprints works differently from mixing colors with acrylic or oil paints. Try a little kitchen magic and tinker with the pH of the ecoprint environment. Brushing on a solution of soda ash (washing soda) or baking soda reduces acidity, raises dye pH, and shifts color in one direction; lemon juice or white vinegar lowers pH and shifts color in another direction. With some plant dyes, pH modifiers can cause dramatic and appealing changes. Color shifts can vary not only according to the plant but also how the plant chemistry responds to the contents of the paper or textile.

To raise pH, start with a solution of ½ teaspoon of soda ash or baking soda in 1 cup of water; brush (splash, drip, stamp, etc.) onto the ecoprint selectively to change the color in just the treated areas.

To lower pH, make a solution of water and lemon juice or vinegar. Apply as above. Experiment with amounts.

2. Using iron modifiers

Introducing iron into ecoprint bundles before or after processing has an overall darkening effect and can also cause prints to "pop." Ferrous sulfate powder and rusty-iron liquor (ferrous acetate) create different color effects.

Ferrous sulfate solution can darken and "greenify" prints and add definition to plant forms. Brush it on or apply it to a dye blanket (dye carrier sheet) before processing. Start with ¼ teaspoon of ferrous sulfate in 1 cup of water.

Left: The generally pink and purple color of wild grape is shifted to teal blues by the high pH of the paper substrate, but acid from a direct print of the lemon shifts the color back to pinks.

PLANTS FOR ECOPRINTING

Plant Name	Part of Plant	Ecoprint Basic Color	Colorplay Tips
Bee balm *Monarda didyma*	petals	pink	Use for heat-processing or plant-pounding
Chokecherry *Prunus virginiana*	leaves	dark charcoal, yellow	Use with iron for extra-dark prints
Coreopsis *Coreopsis lanceolata, C. tinctoria, C. verticillata*	blooms whole plant	orange red-orange	Paint areas with soda ash after printing for red-orange
Common elder *Sambucus canadensis*	berries leaves	purple-blue green	Apply crushed berries before or after printing for blues and purples
Perennial geranium *Geranium macrorrhizum*	leaves	yellow-green	Process with rusted iron bits for black, charcoal, or orange
Goldenrod *Solidago* spp.	blooms leaves	yellow green	Process ecoprint bundle in dyebath to obtain dye color around the edges
Wild grape *Vitis riparia*	ripe fruits	purple-blue, strong pink, blue, gray	1) Apply crushed fruits before or after processing 2) Crush fruit onto unmordanted cloth or paper to use as a dye blanket; color is affected by chemistry of paper 3) Paint areas with soda ash or lemon juice to shift colors (see page 37)
Blue iris *Iris* spp.	blooms	green, turquoise, blue, purple	1) Crush petals onto unmordanted cloth or paper as a green dye blanket 2) Use alum-mordanted substrates and heat-process to obtain the other colors
Japanese maple *Acer palmatum*	red leaves	green, blue, gray	1) Pound for red-purple 2) Heat-process for teal green ecoprints
Sugar maple *Acer saccharum*	leaves	green, brown, yellow	Heat-process with rusted iron bits for charcoal, black, or orange
Marigold *Tagetes* spp.	blooms calices leaves	yellow orange green green	Use for heat-processing, plant-pounding, or dyebath
Oak *Quercus* spp.	leaves	brown, yellow	Use with iron for darker prints
Osage orange *Maclura pomifera*	heartwood shavings or sawdust	warm yellow	1) Sprinkle for strong color or to promote color mixing in the bundle 2) Brush with soda ash solution for deeper color
Purple sand cherry *Prunus cistena*	leaves	dark green (tannin-rich)	Use with iron for darker prints
Smokebush *Cotinus obovatus; C. coggygria*	leaves	green, yellow orange, occasionally blue (tannin-rich)	Use with iron for darker prints
Staghorn sumac *Rhus typhina*	leaves fruits	yellow-green and dark green, red and pink (tannin-rich)	Use with iron for darker prints
Sweet gum *Liquidambar styraciflua*	leaves	yellow, green, occasionally blue (tannin-rich)	Use with iron for darker prints
Black walnut *Juglans nigra*	leaves fruits	dark yellow; occasionally lavender-pink, dark brown (tannin-rich, substantive dye)	1) Use for tannin-rich leaf prints 2) Soak green walnut hulls in water with unmordanted paper or cloth to make a dark brown dye blanket

To color tannin-rich leaves such as sumac, maple, or sweet gum toward black, or to make orange rust prints, selectively brush on rusty-iron liquor and include iron bits in the ecoprint bundle. To make rusty-iron liquor, steep iron nails in vinegar for a few weeks until the solution is orange-colored (see page 81).

3. Coloring ecoprints in a dyebath

Immerse your securely tied ecoprint bundle (paper or cloth) in a dyebath and simmer it along with the dye material. The dye color will seep a little inside the bundle, color the edges of the bundle, and mingle with the ecoprint plants to create new colors.

4. Tinting ecoprints with art materials

Apply watercolor paints, natural plant inks, mineral earth pigments, or other art media to ecoprinted papers to enhance print colors, develop print designs, or add interesting marks. Suitably prepared textile ecoprints can be printed further with dye pastes or painted with textile-appropriate materials. You can use an ecoprint as an inspiration layer in a new, mixed-media artwork.

Above: Black maple leaves printed on silk shift from green to black when heat-processed with ferrous sulfate and a piece of rusted iron.

Bottom left: Orange rust prints and black maple leaf prints on paper, heat-processed with ferrous acetate.
Bottom right: Purple sand cherry leaves create green prints on watercolor paper; in a hibiscus pink dyebath, the colors shift from greens to purple, blue, and teal.

HINTS TO PRESERVE ECOPRINTS

Heat-processed and pounded botanical prints can be prone to fading, but the following precautions may help protect your prints. Some plant colors are certain to change with time, despite efforts at retention.

- Protect ecoprints from direct light.
- Use a casein-based fixative on finished work.
- Apply a coat of natural wax if desired.
- Frame under UV-resistant glass.

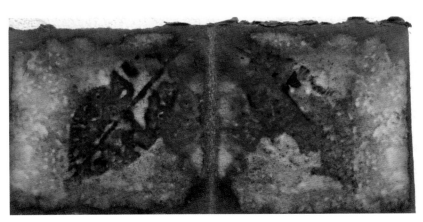

PLANTS FOR POUNDING

The list of plants for pounding will vary from season to season. This is an excellent opportunity to experiment.

The plants used in the samples on page 43 and 44 were available in October:

Calendula marigold whole flower (orange)

Tagetes marigold petals (yellow)

Monarda/bee balm petals (pink)

Clover (green)

Japanese maple windfall leaves (burgundy/purple)

Cornflower petals (blue)

Oregano leaves (green)

Baptisia australis leaves (green)

I select plants for pounding according to color, shape, size, season—and my artist's eye. In addition to the list at left, I suggest geraniums (whole blooms, petals, and leaves) and blue pansy flowers. Many of these colors will likely fade on pounded substrates, especially the chlorophyl from any greens. Prints obtained by this method are probably not washfast.

ECOPRINTING PROJECTS

With an artistic approach and variability in the plants themselves, ecoprinting always involves an element of experimentation. For the best chance of a good result, start with the supplies and equipment that have given consistently good results to successful ecoprinters and natural dyers. Adventure into other materials once you've had success with the basic process.

Rusted iron with sumac, elder, black tea, and indigo on paper, before and after heat-processing on a hot summer day under black plastic resting on hot stones.

PROJECT 1
ECOPRINTED GREETING CARDS

Start an ecoprint adventure with mordanted paper! This method achieves a print in just a few steps by steaming the plants with paper in an ordinary pot. Cover about half of the paper surface with plants contrasting in size, dye color, and shape. Even a first print can be special.

Supplies

- Plant selections
- Two 11" x 15" sheets of 140 lb or 90 lb watercolor paper, each cut to three sheets 5" x 11" and folded in half to make a set of 6 cards, 5" x 5½" (or use commercial blank cards). *Note:* Paper types influence color outcomes.
- Alum acetate as mordant
- Stainless steel, aluminum, or ceramic vessel with a rack or colander to hold the bundles. (Aluminum is okay for steaming but best avoided for dye-baths.)

Steps

1. Dissolve 2 teaspoons of alum acetate in a little hot water; add this to 4 cups of water in a nonreactive container.
2. Soak the cards for 2 hours or longer.
3. Remove the cards. Towel-blot them dry.
4. Open a folded card on a flat surface. Cover half the surface with plants (1). Close the card.

5. Repeat with the remaining five cards.

6. Stack three folded cards on one piece of cardboard. Insert plants between the cards as desired.

7. Cover the stack with a second piece of cardboard. Wrap the bundle tightly with string.

8. Make a second stack of three folded cards.

9. Place the two bundles on the rack or colander inside the steaming vessel (2).

10. Weigh down the stacks with a brick or similar weight.

11. Add water under the rack or colander.

12. Steam the bundles on high heat, covered, for an hour or longer. Top up the water as needed. Turn the bundles every 15–20 minutes. (*Check for color showing along the sides of the bundles. Peeking inside is safe.*)

13. When you are pleased with the color, turn off the heat. Leave the bundles to rest at least until cool.

14. Unwrap the bundles (3), dry the prints, then flatten them under weights.

Above: Layout of lemon gem tagetes marigold, Japanese maple, rose leaf, fern, and bee balm petals. *Right:* Print that includes Japanese maple, coreopsis, and chokecherry.

Left: Revealing the print: Japanese maple, calendula, tagetes, clover, cornflower, and oregano.

PROJECT 2
PLANT-POUNDED ECOPRINT ON COTTON OR LINEN

With adult supervision, minimal equipment, recycled fabric, and maybe a little hammering practice, plant pounding is kid-friendly ecoprinting (1): simply hammer the plants onto mordanted cotton or linen (or opt for watercolor paper and skip scouring). This direct process captures colors well, especially greens; scouring, mordanting, steam-ironing, and air-curing the fabric help to retain colors. It is best not to wash pounded-plant textiles.

Supplies (2)

- Leaves and thin-walled blooms or petals (avoid waxy or juicy plants; cut off bulky parts)
- White or beige cotton or linen fabric (such as a thrift-shop napkin), scoured in boiling water with pH-neutral soap and 1 tablespoon of soda ash, then rinsed and damp-dried
- *Optional:* a second sheet of fabric or piece of watercolor paper to obtain two prints
- Alum acetate as mordant
- Nonreactive (stainless steel or enamel) container for mordanting the fabric
- Parchment paper and masking tape
- Rubber mallet, a small round-headed hammer, and/or flat-headed hammer
- Wooden board to hammer on
- Mask and gloves for handling materials

Steps

1. Dissolve 2 teaspoons of alum acetate in a little hot water; add this to 4 cups of water in the nonreactive container.
2. Soak the fabric for 2 hours or longer.
3. After soaking, rinse well and damp-dry.
4. Place parchment paper on the wood board with the fabric on top.

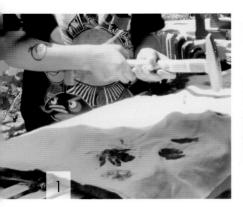

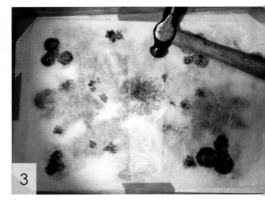

5. Lay plants randomly or in a design on the fabric. Place petals sun side down; place leaves vein side down.

6. Secure papers and plants with masking tape as necessary.

7. Fold fabric or place a second piece of fabric or watercolor paper over the plants to obtain a mirror-image print.

8. Place parchment paper on top of the plant "sandwich."

9. Hammer with gradually increasing force (3). Try the larger, flatter mallet followed by the smaller hammers.

10. Turn the sandwich over. Continue pounding until a clear image appears.

11. Rub off the plants gently; dry the fabric.

12. Steam-iron the fabric (print side down on parchment paper) on the highest setting for about 5 minutes.

13. Hang the print(s) out of direct light for a week to cure.

14. Sign your work and frame it!

HARVESTING PLANTS FOR ECOPRINTING

- "Natural" is not a synonym for "safe" or "healthy." Some plants are toxic for everyone; some cause reactions in a few people only. Be diligent and do your own research. Check online for lists of toxic local or regional plants. When in doubt, do not touch, and avoid breathing in pollen.
- Forage for plants with reference materials in hand or bring a knowledgeable companion.
- Be aware of local ordinances regarding plant collection. Gather no more than 10 percent of plants at any one stand in the wild; gather only windfalls in public parks (and only windfall lichens).
- Invasive plants such as privet (*Ligustrum* spp.), buckthorn (*Rhamnus cathartica*) or woad (*Isatis tinctoria*) are interesting sources of natural dye color, but check local regulations, which may prohibit gathering for fear of unintentional propagation.
- Wear cover-up clothing while foraging.
- Use copper as a bundling rod for ecoprints or as a dyepot; avoid using copper acetate as modifier.

ECOPRINT ARTISTS

THESE THREE ARTISTS have inspired me to take new steps in my own ecoprinting adventures. Their unique interpretations show some of the exciting developments in ecoprinting as an art genre.

Irit Dulman
iritdulman.com, @iritdulman

I approach cloth and plants as imaginative records of personal place and culture. Inspired and guided by the shapes, colors, and properties of plants, I ecoprint textiles as art to be worn. I am always learning what to expect from my materials as I work, allowing them to guide me in achieving compositions of striking color, form, and contrast.

Right: Kimono, colored with Virginia creeper and *Combretum indicum.*
Photo courtesy of Irit Dulman

Jane Dunnewold
janedunnewold.com, @jane.dunnewold

In my recently developed and unorthodox approach, I use a heat press to print botanicals primarily on paper. Drawing on an extensive repertoire of surface-design processes, including fiber-reactive dyes, gold leaf, matte medium, and Inktense crayons, I collaborate with the infinite beauty of foliage and flowers, adding color and depth to my botanical prints in a distinctive way.

Left: Eucalyptus Study.
Photo courtesy of Jane Dunnewold

Rose L. Williams
roselwilliamsarts.com, @rose_l_williams

In my mixed-media art, creativity, insight, and imagination heal and transform trauma. Inspired by life-sustaining flora and fauna, I dye and print with plants that carry potent contexts of domestic technology, botanical medicine, and historical considerations. Plants and dyes can be imbued with my own personal cultural symbolism or another's. One grandma's genteel vintage linen can reprise another's connection to logwood dye and slavery.

Right: Buck Deer in Forest Fire on cotton.
Photo courtesy of Rose L. Williams

A dye garden can be as simple as a few pots of marigolds, zinnias, and cosmos—maybe even Japanese indigo—on a sunny patio. Or you can go big, join with others, and create a garden to serve a whole community with inspiration and color. Donna Brown describes the project she and her weavers' guild undertook, in partnership with the Denver Botanic Gardens, and the spectacular and sustainable results they've achieved.

Photo by Janét Bare

LET US NOT
dye alone

Donna Brown

THOSE OF US WHO LOVE TO CREATE color from plants can point to a host of reasons. For some of us, the major draw is the glorious palette of colors. For others, it's the personal and artistic satisfaction of gathering plant material and transforming it into color on fiber. Learning about the historical significance associated with plant dyeing and keeping traditions alive is also fulfilling. Most of us could say "all of the above" to explain our interest, but there's even more: sharing with the unsuspecting public the alchemy of converting green plants into a veritable rainbow of hues.

When Janice Ford died in 2011, her family memorialized her by making a substantial donation to the Rocky Mountain Weavers' Guild (RMWG). I had been thinking that a dye garden would be a perfect addition to Denver Botanic Gardens' Chatfield Farms, which is a 740-acre homestead in Littleton, Colorado. Chatfield Farms includes the original home, a cutting garden, an herb garden, a vegetable-market garden, and a 5-acre community-supporting-agriculture garden. I cold-called the director of the Denver Botanic Gardens (DBG), Larry Vickerman, about the possibility. He immediately embraced the idea of forming a collaboration between DBG and RMWG to create a dye garden. It was agreed that DBG would provide labor to prepare the garden and fencing and would also start the seeds in its greenhouse. The RMWG group agreed to do the planting, weeding, harvesting, and drying of the dye material. And that's what we've been doing for seven years now.

With the go-ahead from the DBG, we formed a study group. We immediately went to work researching dye plants and making decisions about what the Janice Ford Memorial Dye Garden would look like. We selected a sunny spot that had previously been a seed garden; it also had nearby water access for irrigation. Our plant selection included annuals and perennials that had the potential of yielding a variety of colors. A number of garden dye plants give yellow, so we knew we wanted to add indigo for blue and madder for Turkey red. We selected some plants native to our Western region, such

Left: Photo by Scott Dressel-Martin; right: Photo by Catherine Jacobus

Left: Multitiered drying racks make short work of preparing dye materials for storage in Denver's arid climate.

Right: An outdoor kitchen makes preparing a weekly community dyepot easy.

as cota and Hopi sunflowers. We planted black hollyhocks (an heirloom variety) to honor the DBG homestead and its history. Popular garden ornamentals such as marigolds, cosmos, and black-eyed Susans were included to educate the public about their use as dye plants.

Over the years, the RMWG garden group has grown to 30 members. Most of our work takes place in the summer, when 12 to 15 members gather once a week to maintain the garden. During a typical summer, we've logged 1,200 volunteer hours. We have access to a historic granary building in which to store our equipment and dye material; flowers in full bloom are picked weekly and put onto a drying rack consisting of layers of mesh (above left). Colorado is quite dry, so in only a week the dried flowers are ready to be stored and labeled in lidded plastic containers. Each week, we have a community dyepot for dyeing yarn or fabric for our personal projects.

To heat the dyepot, we set up camp stoves near the garden, or we use an outdoor kitchen that is nearby. Visitors to the garden enjoy seeing these dyeing demonstrations.

The location of the garden has been critical to its success. Most dye plants do not do well in shade; full sunshine is best, or at least six hours of direct sun. Any garden shape will do, but having good access to all the plants is important. The size of the garden is also important. Our dye garden is 1,500 square feet—large enough to represent each plant type, but not so large that our group gets overwhelmed with maintaining the garden. We typically plant 24 to 36 plants of each variety, but our indigo plants—Japanese indigo, *Persicaria tinctoria*—cover a large space with more than 120 plants. We have kept to a simple plan: five linear rows of raised beds with mulched walking paths in between and more beds along the fencing. This allows for easy placement of the irrigation tubing and easy access to the plants, both for our volunteers and for the public.

Our dye garden offers many community outreach opportunities. The DBG holds camp sessions for kids for six weeks in the summer, and for each session, we do a special project. For example, we have dyed bandannas with marigolds, along with taking the kids on a garden tour and teaching them about the dye plants and colors they yield (bottom left). Our group also spends a day each summer with the

Left: Japanese indigo yields many shades of blue and turquoise.

Below left: Kids love to dye their bandannas with marigold in a summer workshop.

Below right: Guild member Paul Tracy shows the tapestry he wove to highlight colors from the garden and identify their sources for visitors.

Left: Photo by Donna Brown; bottom left: Photo by Catherine Jacobus; bottom right: Photo by Donna Brown

Gallery of yarn samples with their dye plants

Coreopsis

Hopi Sunflower

Cosmos

Japanese Indigo

Illustrations by Ann Sabin Swanson; photos by Joe Coca

Cota

Madder

Marigold

Weld

Black Hollyhock

Left: Photo by Scott Dressel-Martin; right: Photo by Donna Brown

Left: Members of the Rocky Mountain Weavers' Guild do more than weave—they grow color!

Right: Here are just a few of the hues the garden has produced.

DBG horticulture staff so they can understand what we're about. When the DBG holds public events, such as a free day each month or an annual lavender festival, our group sets up a series of demonstrations, including a weaving and spinning station along with naturally dyed samples to show. Our garden has been a popular tour destination with groups such as the Rocky Mountain Unit of the American Herb Society and the Perennial Plant Association. We've held continuing education workshops for the community, too.

One of our members, Paul Tracy, is a tapestry weaver. He's woven a tapestry using the colors produced from the dye garden in the first five years (see photo on page 49), and it hangs in the visitor's center as living, vibrant proof of the magic of natural dyes.

You don't need a relationship with a big horticultural institution such as the Denver Botanic Gardens to plant a dye garden, though. You or your group can partner with state extension facilities, historic sites, or other organizations. I have been able to give financial help for starting a dye garden at John C. Campbell Folk School in Brasstown, North Carolina—the Cory Brown Memorial Dye Garden, named after our son, whom we lost in 2019. The folk school was founded to nurture and preserve the folk arts of the Appalachian Mountains, so a dye garden was a natural fit.

Or you can do it on your own. All you need is a bit of space and gardening know-how, and the desire to connect to an activity rooted in history.

Some common dye plants, growing zones, and the colors they produce

Common Name	Latin Name	Longevity	USDA Zones	Parts to Use	Dye Color
Black-eyed Susan	*Rudbeckia fulgida*	perennial	4 to 9	flowers	yellow-green
Black hollyhock	*Alcea rosea nigra*	biennial	2 to 9	flowers	purple
Cota, Navajo tea	*Thelesperma filifolium*	perennial	4 to 8	flowers	orange
Cosmos, yellow, orange, or red	*Cosmos bipinnatus*	annual	all	flowers	yellow-orange-red
Dahlia	*Dahlia* hybrids	tender perennial	all	flowers	yellow-light orange
Dyer's broom	*Genista tinctoria*	perennial	4 to 7	stems, leaves, flowers	yellow
Dyer's chamomile	*Anthemis tinctoria*	perennial	4 to 6	leaves, flowers	yellow
Dyer's coreopsis or tickseed	*Coreopsis tinctoria*	perennial	all	flowers	yellow-light orange
Goldenrod	*Solidago* spp.	perennial	4 to 8	leafy shoots, flowers	yellow
Hibiscus or rose mallow	*Hibiscus* spp.	deciduous shrub	4 to 9	shoots	purple or green
Hops	*Humulus lupulus*	perennial	3 to 8	tops, roots	tan-yellow
Japanese indigo	*Persicaria tinctoria*	frost-tender annual	all	leaves, flowers	blue
Lady's bedstraw or cleavers	*Galium verum*	perennial	3 to 8	leaves, flowers	yellow-orange
Madder	*Rubia tinctoria*	perennial	5 to 9	roots	red-orange
Marigold, African	*Tagetes erecta*	annual	all	flowers	yellow
Marigold, French	*Tagetes patula*	annual	all	flowers	yellow
Marigold, Mexican	*Tagetes lucida*	annual	all	flowers	yellow
St. John's wort	*Hypericum perforatum*	perennial	5 to 10	flowers or whole plant	tan-gold
Sunflower	*Helianthus annuus*	annual	all	flowers	yellow
Tansy	*Tanacetum vulgare*	perennial	3 to 9	whole plant tops	yellow
Weld	*Reseda luteola*	biennial or perennial	5 to 9	first year, leaves; second year, whole flower stalks	yellow
Yellow yarrow	*Achillea* spp.	perennial	4 to 8	leaves and flower stalks	light yellow

lichens for dyes

Alissa Allen

"Knowing that you love the earth changes you, activates you to defend and protect and celebrate. But when you feel that the earth loves you in return, that feeling transforms the relationship from a one-way street into a sacred bond."

Robin Wall Kimmerer, Braiding Sweetgrass: Indigenous Wisdom, Scientific Knowledge, and the Teaching of Plants

IT'S NO WONDER humans are drawn to natural dyeing. There is something primal and mysterious about collecting material from the wild, stirring it into a pot of boiling water, and watching as the mixture transforms fibers from their natural color to a vibrant hue. People are curious and fascinated by color-changing chemistry. As early as childhood—from mixing potions of flower petals and water in the garden, to secretly loving the emerald of grass stains on jeans—colorful dyes are part of our collective human experience. We all have the urge to be creative on some level, and natural dyeing is a wonderful way to satisfy this inclination. It is a special art form that does not require any developed talent or ability, yet it allows us to take fragments of nature that would otherwise return to earth and transform them into useful, tangible, and beautiful textiles that will last through time.

Some of those transformative bits and pieces are the inconspicuous little tufts, bumps, and leaflike organisms that are lichens. Lichens are capable of making some of the most brilliant colors: burnt orange, neon yellow, rich shades of gold and amber, and a range of earthy browns. More surprisingly, they also make hot pink, sky blue, and most notably, magenta and purple. Lichen dyes have been used throughout history, dating back at least 2,000 years. Remnants of ancient parchments and textiles from as early as the third century CE have been found to contain purple lichen dyes. Lichens are culturally significant dye sources that have been in continuous use, both casually and ceremonially, in cultures all over the world, through modern times.

Many modern natural dyers shy away from exploring lichens because of concerns of overharvest and accidental harvest of rare species. These are valid concerns. In the past, certain species were overharvested to the point of extinction when the demand for lichen-dyed cloth outpaced the slow life cycle of the organism. However, by familiarizing yourself with the life cycle and ecology of lichens, and by committing to the simple set of guidelines outlined, exploring lichens for dyeing can be an ethical and accessible craft for all interested in lichens and their use as dye.

Opposite: Lichens can take on many different forms. Here you see examples of foliose, fruticose, and crustose.

Photos by the author unless otherwise indicated

Above: Mixed lichens: foliose, fruticose, crustose.

people all over the world who upload pictures and descriptions of their nature observations (plants, animals, fungi, and such). As a user, you can add your own observation, peruse others' observations, and find mentorship in your region and area of interest. Once you hone your identification skills, you can help others identify their observations.

To get you started, I've compiled a list of reasonably common and abundant species and the regions where you might find them.

LEARNING ABOUT LICHENS

Mastering lichen identification takes years of study, but learning common local species is something anyone can grasp. The best ways to get started with lichen identification are by getting a field guide, by joining a discussion group such as Lichens Connecting People! on Facebook, and most importantly, by contributing observations through a science-based community reporting site such as iNaturalist.

Any lichen field guide will introduce you to the basics of identification. A guide with pictures and descriptions specific to your part of the world will be more helpful if you're using it for photo matching, so get something regional if possible. Books will present you with the basics, but getting feedback from more experienced lichen enthusiasts will take you further. Facebook groups are active areas of discussion on lichens, but identification requests often go unanswered, which can be frustrating. The web-based database iNaturalist is driven by

SOME COMMON LICHENS BY REGION *Verify data with iNaturalist*	Pacific Northwest	Southwest, California, Rockies	Midwest to Southeast	East/Northeast
Evernia Srunastri	x	x		
Flavopunctelia flaventior		x		x
*Lasallia papulosa				x
Letharia spp.	x	x		
Lobaria pulmonaria	x			
Ochrolechia spp.	x			
Parmotrema spp.		x	x	
Pseudevernia spp.			x	
Punctelia rudecta/ subrudecta		x	x	x
Teloschistes spp.			x	
*Umbilicaria mammulata				x
Usnea spp.	x	x	x	x
Vulpicida spp.	x	x		
Xanthoria parietina	x	x	x	x

*These lichens are very slow growing—extreme care should be taken when interfacing with them and teaching about them.

LICHEN BASICS

Before diving into dyeing with lichens, let's talk about lichens themselves: what they are and how to describe them to others.

Lichens can be found in almost any habitat: forests, beaches, prairies, deserts, mountains, and urban areas. They grow on all kinds of substrates: tree bark, stone, man-made structures, stumps, and directly from the soil. They can be very particular about where they grow—some prefer to be high in the forest canopy, others close to the trunk of a tree. Some are only found on certain types of rocks, while others will grow just about anywhere. Most have very specific environmental requirements; if they are disrupted, they will fail to thrive and eventually decompose.

Because lichens are particularly sensitive to air pollution and they need water to thrive, scientists look to them as bioindicators. Lichens are making a comeback in some areas as the air gets cleaned up, but they are disappearing from other areas as climate change intensifies. Lichens are generally less diverse in areas of drought, areas impacted by agricultural runoff, and industrial zones.

Lichens are compound organisms made up of **fungi** and a **photobiont** such as green algae, or sometimes cyanobacteria (also known as blue-green algae). These organisms live mutualistically in one body; the photobiont can offer the green or gray colors often seen in lichens, and it provides nutrients from photosynthesis to the fungi. In turn, the fungal component provides housing for the photobiont. The rest of the lichens' needs are met through absorbing minerals from moisture and air. Though they share some characteristics with plants, the fungal component is responsible for reproduction. Therefore, lichens are classified as members of the Fungal Kingdom.

It is the responsibility of the dyer to harvest ethically and also to teach others to do the same.

Lichens are extremely slow growing, relying on moisture rather than the seasons to proliferate. Care must be taken to ensure they are harvested more conscientiously than vascular plants or mushrooms. The following code of ethics is adapted from the work of Karen Diadick Casselman in *Lichen Dyes: The New Source Book*. This book is a must-have for anyone interested in lichens and their use as dye.

Ethical Harvest of Lichens

1. **Get a lichen identification guide and read up on lichen ecology and reproduction.** Learn to identify a few common lichens before approaching them for dyes.
2. **Only collect locally abundant lichens.** Base your dyeing on what is available, not the color you want to make.
3. **Only collect lichens that are detached from their happy growing place.** This can look like firewood, windfallen branches, pieces crumbled off rocks by natural elements, and lichens detached due to land clearing, development, or other human activity. Keep in mind that some lichens are perfectly happy growing from the ground, on stumps, or draped in shrubs, making the differentiation more difficult. When in doubt, let it grow.
4. **Leave 90% or more undisturbed.** Lichens provide nutrients to the soil and hiding places for critters; leave plenty behind.
5. **Do not collect in protected areas.** This includes historical sites and areas where their collection is prohibited.
6. **Lichens should not be sold for dye purposes.** Commodifying a slow-growing natural resource eventually leads to overharvest. Some lichens are so old that they were born under different conditions. Though their colony is hanging on, the conditions to start over may not exist.

is almost always some level of flatness to them, and they are usually different colors on top and bottom (green and white, green and brown, or green and black). Fruticose lichens are shrubby like miniature fruit trees; they often stand upright, are branching, and are the same color all the way around. Crustose lichens form a crust on the substrate and are not leafy or something that peels up. Crustose lichens are not used for dye—they are fused to the rock or bark on which they reside.

Lichens come in a broad assortment of colors: golden-green, chartreuse, bright orange, rusty red, and even crimson; but most can be described as mineral green (think green clay, like the kind used in beauty masks). When the weather is dry, they often look pastel or gray, contrasting with the vibrant green of plants and mosses and making it easy to identify them. But after a good rain, many turn green, making their color a less reliable distinguishing characteristic. Beyond color, the easiest way to distinguish them from plants and mosses is by their lack of stems and leaves and by the presence of reproductive structures that look like disks.

The body of the lichen is called the **thallus.** The thallus comes in three distinct shapes or forms: **foliose, fruticose,** or **crustose.** One trick to remembering these descriptors is to associate them with other words that sound similar. Foliose means leaf-like—similar to the word foliage. Foliose lichens are made up of leafy lobes that often lie flat on their **substrate** (the place they grow); the lobes are sometimes simple, without branching, or they may be complex, with lots of branching. There

The thallus is made up of several layers, the **upper cortex,** the **photobiont layer,** the inner fungal layer called the **medulla,** and the **lower cortex.** The real magic of dye production takes place in the interior of the lichen, the region called the medulla. The medulla is made up entirely of fungal tissue and is where the dye chemicals exist. When we do chemical spot tests, this is the area dyers need to access for results.

Apothecia are sexual reproductive structures of the fungal component of lichen. They are usually cup-shaped and often a contrasting color from the body (sometimes bright or dark, and occasionally similar to the thallus). Sexual reproduction of the lichen occurs with rain. The cuplike structures unfold and become active shortly after rehydration. When dry, the apothecia can be hard to see (a handheld lens will help). Recognizing the presence or absence of these structures is helpful for identification.

Some lichens have rootlike appendages called **rhizines** that come from the bottom of certain leafy-shaped, foliose lichens. Their presence or absence can help you narrow down what genus you are looking at. Somewhat similar in shape, thinner hairlike appendages called **cilia** that resemble eyelashes can also be present along the margin of lobes or the edges of the apothecia. These hairy, rootlike structures provide stability and are not vascular. Being able to recognize and describe them is essential for identification.

Exploring lichens through dyeing makes learning about them easier. When you have context and an application, you are driven to find them in their habitat, understand their chemistry, and recognize their abundance or scarcity. From a community science perspective, this is important because the study of lichens is underrepresented compared to that of animals and plant life. It is human nature to care for the underdog, and lichens certainly fill the ranks of neglected organisms in the world of biological study. When you value these lesser-appreciated elements of nature, you inherently want to pass your knowledge and concern on to the next generation, creating a starting point for making progress in the biological sciences.

GETTING STARTED

Not all lichens make dye, but many do, and they are easy to test. Unlike plant dyes that come with recipes and relatively consistent results, lichen dyes are less predictable and underdocumented. Because there is no standard expectation, you can experiment freely without the fear of making a mistake. You don't even have to be able to identify the lichens. As long as you can visually verify that they are, in fact, abundant, common, and detached from their happy growing place, you can explore them for color.

Lichen dyes, like many natural-dye sources, tend to be more brilliant on wool and silk. Unlike other dye sources, lichens contain their own acids, which act similarly to mordants. With plant and mushroom dyeing, mordants such as alum and iron are used to increase lightfastness and/or to bring about color change, but interestingly, lichen-dyed fibers are not enhanced by these additions and do better without them.

Lichen dyes extracted with water alone are permanent and have strong staying power. This technique is referred to as **BWM,** or the **Boiling Water Method.** Lichen dyes extracted this way often impart a sweet, earthy fragrance that is permanently laced into the fiber.

A small percentage of lichens make an electric purple dye after a lengthy soak in ammonia (historically, stale urine was used). This method is called the **Ammonia Method,** or **AM** for short. The purple dye is more sensitive to sunlight and will fade with direct exposure over time; however, it is totally worth exploring and celebrating the brilliant magenta color that is unparalleled

Left: Note the small cuplike structures, the sexual reproductive structures of lichens.

in the natural-dye world. Lichens that contain the chemistry that makes purple dye are less common and at highest risk for overharvest, so utmost respect and care must be given when working with them and promoting their use.

To transform a greenish lichen to purple dye, you must first find the lichens that contain the chemical precursors that can do that. The lichens that make purple dye are green, so until you can recognize them by sight, you must rely on chemical spot-testing to tell them apart from the multitudes of similar-looking species. Luckily, the dye chemicals are reactive to chlorine bleach and can quickly be identified with a drop placed on the inner tissue of the lichen, the medulla. This is where I like to start with any unfamiliar lichen: first, **rule out purple.**

TESTING

Before you do anything, snap a few pictures and make note of all characteristics: shape, color, and texture; presence or absence of apothecia, rhizines, and cilia; and habitat and substrate. Then proceed with testing.

Chlorine test (C-test): You can test a lichen that is wet or dry, fresh or stored; the chemistry is stable. Take a sample of ethically harvested lichen (abundant, detached) and gently scrape away the outer layer. This works best using a knife tip or fingernail on a moistened lichen. You want to scrape away the outer layer of color on the lichen to reveal the inner white tissue. This is the fungal hyphal layer where the dye chemicals reside. Once you get to the white chalky innards, apply a drop of fresh chlorine bleach. The lichen's reaction will depend on the presence or absence of certain lichen acids.

Right: The tiny bright pink dot on this *Punctelia rudecta* is the result of a drop of chlorine bleach, showing its potential as a purple dye.

For the magenta dye lichens, you are looking for a **bright red or pink reaction;** this is noted as C+ if red or C− if there is no reaction. A C+ result indicates the presence of purple dye components that will slowly transform into magenta dye in the presence of ammonia. If there is no color change, or a yellow reaction, there is no need for ammonia and no likelihood of a purple result; continue to the boiling water test. Exceptions are *Evernia* and *Pseudevernia*, which are C− but are processed as though they are C+.

Boiling water test: The boiling water test is as easy as it sounds. Use about four times the amount of lichen as fiber being tested. I do this by eyeballing the volume: For testing, I use about four generous pinches of lichen to a 6-inch piece of wool yarn. Add just enough water to keep the fiber and lichen covered and moving freely throughout the process. Aim for a sustained simmer of about 180°F for a minimum of one hour. *Note:* The color of the lichen and dyebath might have nothing to do with the outcome of the dye test. The lichen may be

pale green and the water nearly clear, yet the result might be saturated and colorful.

If the color change is not impressive after the boiling water test and there was no color change with the chlorine test, you can file your lichen away as a **nondye species.**

DYEING PROCESS

Boiling Water Method (BWM)

When working with a boiling water extraction, start with at least 2 parts lichen to 1 part fiber. This can be measured by the weight of lichen relative to the weight of the fiber, or if you don't have access to a scale, you can measure by volume. A higher lichen-to-fiber ratio will give a more saturated result, so go bold by adding more lichen if you have the quantity and desire to do so. Leftover dye can be used for dyeing a second or third exhaust bath that will yield softer colors.

For a solid dye color, chop the lichen into dime-sized pieces with scissors. Contain the bits in a mesh bag to keep them out of your fiber.

If time permits, cover your fiber and lichen with water and soak overnight, or just get started by adding it all together and bringing it to 160°F to 200°F. A pinch of ordinary table salt added to the dyebath is said to help stabilize the color, though I suspect this may be superstition. Regardless, it doesn't seem to hurt.

If you prefer a mottled yarn, use less water and slow-cook the fiber in a wet slurry of lichens, allowing the pieces to press against the fiber. This technique should be kept under careful watch, on low heat in a double boiler, so the

fiber doesn't burn. The results will be a gorgeous, richly speckled yarn.

After your yarn has simmered for an hour, let the dyebath cool, yarn and all—at this point, you can consider it done. Remove the fiber from the bath, shake out any lichen pieces, and let it dry without rinsing. Before use, rinse the yarn gently and air-dry. Delaying the rinse is said to increase the staying power of the dye.

Stacking the color: If time permits, you may be able to extract more color by reheating the dyebath along with the fiber and simmering it again. You can repeat this heating and cooling process for days, for an increasingly saturated result.

Ammonia Method (AM)

If the lichen tests positive with chlorine for purple-dye components (the scratched area will turn red or pink for a moment), do an ammonia extraction. This process takes at least six weeks but is well worth the effort. There is nothing as vibrant as an ammonia-extracted magenta dye.

Above: Dyeing skeins of yarn in the same pot with mixed windfall lichens results in an attractive marbling effect.

GUIDE TO COMMON LICHENS

Lobaria pulmonaria Lungwort

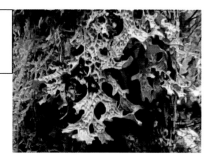

Distribution: Alaska to central coast of California, east to Montana and Canadian Rockies, the Great Lakes region, and northeastern North America.

Description: Large, leafy lichen that grows in clusters with ridges and pits and a scooped look to its edges. Upper surface is pale gray when dry, turning bright green when wet. Underside is white with tan venations. Apothecia are reddish brown if present.

Habitat: Grows where the air is clean, most often attached to mossy tree trunks and branches. Collect from windfall or from the ground.

Boiling water extraction/dye process: Use fresh, or dry for later use. Follow Boiling Water Method, page 61. After simmer and cool sessions, rinse and allow to dry; it is ready for use.

Colors to expect: Warm brown, deep orange, gold.

Usnea species Cord lichen

Distribution: Worldwide.

Description: Can be easily identified to genus by the unifying feature of the central cord. It is fruticose, bushy, and branching, often growing in a beard-like fashion. It is most often pale green but sometimes bluish green or orange-red depending on species and conditions. It can be rare in some areas but can flourish after becoming detached if draped in branches. Avoid *U. longissimi*, recognized by the length to which it grows.

Habitat: Found on all types of surfaces, but look for it on windfall and firewood.

Boiling water extraction/dye process: Use fresh, or dry for later use. Follow Boiling Water Method, page 61. The dyebath may not change color, but yarn will still take up dye. After simmer and cool sessions, rinse and allow to dry; it is ready for use.

Colors to expect: Warm brown, deep orange, gold.

Letharia species Wolf lichen

Distribution: Common in montane areas of western North America.

Description: Bright neon yellow/green bushy fruticose lichens.

Habitat: Grows on conifers, often at higher elevations. You know you are in a good collection zone when this lichen is scattered across the forest floor. Collect from windfall, fallen trees, and off the ground. Use fresh, or dry for later use.

Boiling water extraction/dye process: Follow Boiling Water Method, page 61. A honey-like fragrance permeates the fiber indefinitely.

Colors to expect: Neon yellow to gold.

Distribution: *Punctelia rudecta* is abundant in the eastern half of the United States; *P. subrudecta* is common in the Northeast, southern Rockies, and on the west coast.

Description: These two species look similar: dark grayish-green foliose lichens dotted with punctations and white spots on the surface of the thallus. Underside is tan and slightly fuzzy. Medulla is C+.

Habitat: Common on trees and branches; tolerant of pollution so can be found in urban areas. Collect from windfall and firewood.

Ammonia extraction process: Soak in ammonia until liquid turns the color of red wine or grape juice.

Dye process: Follow Ammonia Method, page 61.

Colors to expect: Bright to dark magenta.

Punctelia rudecta/ subrudecta
Punctate Shield Lichen

Distribution: Common and abundant in the southwestern United States, the southern Rockies, the Canadian Rockies, the Great Lakes region, and the Northeast.

Description: Yellow-green foliose lichen with punctations and cracks in the upper surface of the thallus. Edges of the lobes have frequent crescents of powder that are asexual reproductive structures. Underside is slightly fuzzy, black with brown edges. Medulla is C+.

Habitat: Common on bark of all kinds. Collect from windfall and firewood.

Ammonia extraction process: Soak in ammonia until liquid turns the color of red wine or grape juice.

Dye process: Follow Ammonia Method, page 61.

Colors to expect: Magenta to brilliant purple.

Flavopunctelia flaventior
Speckled greenshield

Distribution: All over North America and Europe; thrives in phosphorus-rich areas, farmlands, coastlines, and cities; often abundant where there are bird droppings.

Description: Foliose lichen that grows flat or bubbled up on wood, bark, or stone. It is deeply orange in dry exposed areas but chartreuse-green when wet or in shaded habitats.

Habitat: Branches, stone, and man-made structures. Collect from windfall or firewood; leave on stone, living trees, and man-made structures.

Ammonia extraction process: Scrape lichen from bark when wet. This ammonia-extracted dye changes from pink to blue in sunlight (photo-oxidation). It is potent, so you only need to fill a quart jar halfway with loose lichen. Follow directions for Ammonia Method, page 61. The dye is ready when it is the color of cranberry juice.

Dye process: Add 1–2 ounces of fiber to the jar and let soak in a dark area at room temperature. After one week, rinse outdoors in the evening and dry in darkness to retain pink color or dry in sunlight to shift to blue. Rewet and expose to sunlight again a few times if you live in northern regions. The color shift happens only when fiber is wet.

Xanthoria parietina
Common sunburst lichen

Start by loosely filling a nonreactive vessel with the lichen. I like to use glass so I can easily see the color as it develops. If you have only a little bit of lichen, use a small jar, but if you have a lot, go for a half gallon. Chop the lichen with scissors and place it in the jar—it will shrink down, but that's okay as long as it's loose to start. Cover the chopped lichen with household ammonia and shake to aerate the solution. Shake it daily for one week. After that you can top off the jar with water. Leave an inch or so of air at the top; oxygen is an essential part of the transformative process. If you are pressed for time and can't shake it daily or need to add the water and ammonia all at once, know that it's a pretty forgiving process and it will likely develop just fine. Put the extract in the warmest place in the house—light exposure does not seem to matter, but temperature does.

After 30 to 90 days, your AM vat should have transformed to a deep red-purple. There is no set time for this change to take place—it varies from batch to batch. Rather than looking at the number of days, it's most reliable to go by the color in the jar. Once your extract looks like grape juice (think of the color of syrupy wine or Concord grape drink), it is ready to use. Take about 1 cup of dye liquor per 1 ounce of yarn for a brilliant, saturated result.

Be sure to work outdoors with this dye, as the ammonia vapors are a strong irritant and toxic to breathe. Submerge your fiber into the diluted lichen extract, adding just enough water so that the fiber can move freely. Simmer the mix at 165°F to 180°F for an hour, watching carefully and replenishing the water as necessary. This dye works best extracted hot. A cold soak will not do it justice, so heat it up.

If time permits, **stack the color** by doing the heat-and-cool cycle over the course of a few days. When the fiber is finally pulled from the vat, allow it to dry unrinsed. Delaying the rinse is said to increase the staying power of the dye.

Photo-Oxidizing Dye (POD)

Lichens with xanthoric acid are usually orange-chartreuse with orange apothecia. These lichens have the special capability of making color-shifting dye that is first pink but changes to blue after sun exposure. Lichens that have this capability are easily identified by their orange color, so there is no need for a chlorine test. *Xanthoria parietina* is one of the most ubiquitous of these lichens. It is found at all altitudes, in cities, on countrysides, by the sea, and in arid regions. It is a foliose lichen that is easily collected by scraping it off windfallen sticks, fallen trees, or firewood. It is a strong dye maker.

Right: Two lichens transformed by ammonia and ready for use: *Teloschistes exilis,* a photo-oxidizing dye, and *Umbilicaria mammulata,* a magenta dye maker.

Left: These yarn samples hint at the wide range of colors lurking in lichens, those easily over-looked members of the natural world.

GIVING AND RECEIVING

There are many benefits to dyeing with lichens. Besides the unparalleled richness of the colors themselves, foraging activates our minds, invigorates our bodies, and connects us with the natural world. Paying attention to small and inconspicuous things while breathing clean fresh air slows us down and does wonders for our well-being. Creating a textile using dye goods collected from nature allows us to weave together the essence of place and time. It is a documentation of color, a contract of respect, and a mutually beneficial engagement.

When we incorporate lichen dyeing into our creative process, we are tapping into an ancient practice that enlivens natural fibers with uncommon color and also sets a framework for exploring the workings of one tiny aspect of what nature has to offer. Lichen dyeing is an exploration; it is art, science, and environmental stewardship wrapped into one beautiful package. Your regional dye palette may be heavy in certain colors, lack colors you wish you had, or be sparse compared to other regions, but it is a beautiful unique gift; embrace it—it is yours.

The scale contains stannous chloride, a mordant commonly called tin. *On slate, counterclockwise from bottom left:* Iron nails, copper pennies, aluminum acetate, and potassium aluminum sulfate.

Photo by Joe Coca

mordants

FACTS AND MYTHS

Catharine Ellis

THE WORD "MORDANT" has different meanings in the English language. The root of the word comes from the Latin *modere,* which means "to bite" or "to sting." It can mean a "dark or critical quality" as in "a mordant sense of humor." In music, a *mordent* is a symbol for rapid alternation of notes, but it has the same Latin root word.

As dyers, we are most interested in the Merriam-Webster definition: "a chemical that fixes a dye in or on a substance by combining with the dye to form an insoluble compound." Yet I have found that the word mordant means different things, even to dyers. I am going to try to define the term as it applies to natural dyeing, explore its uses, and dispel a few myths.

My first experience with the use of natural dyes, many years ago, was during a period that I spent studying on the Navajo reservation in Arizona. There, we gathered plant materials for color and alum mordant from deposits on the surface of the ground. The Arizona mountains are one of few places where these alum deposits exist, and today, they are carefully protected for use by the Navajo weavers and dyers. We placed the plant material, the alum, and the wool yarn together into the same pot and applied heat to complete the dye process.

That experience in Arizona was a number of years ago. In the meantime, a long career in textiles led me to work with various types of synthetic and some natural dyes. Twelve years ago, I began a focused return to natural dyeing for my own work and immersed myself in the process. Initially, I was thoroughly confused about mordants. In addition to comments about the mineral mordants, I began hearing and reading other conflicting statements: "Use tannin as a mordant." "You can mordant with rhubarb leaves." "Soy milk acts as a mordant."

It took me a while to sort it out. I did lots of research and experimentation, and I sought out teachers. I could not have confidently come to conclusions without the support of and collaboration with my colleague Joy Boutrup, a textile chemist and engineer from Denmark. Joy did her graduate work many years ago in Germany, studying with Helmut Schweppe who wrote the very highly regarded book *Handbuch der Naturfarbstoffe* (Handbook of Natural Dyes). Unfortunately for many of us, this book was never translated from German to English.

Photos by Matt Graves

Above left:
Cloth dyed in a stainless steel pot, yarn dyed in a copper pot (light), and yarn dyed in an iron pot (dark), all dyed with weld.

Above right:
Wool fabric and yarn, all premordanted with alum and dyed with cochineal; *from left:* dyed in a stainless steel pot with a small amount of tin added to the dyebath; dyed in a stainless steel pot; dyed in an iron pot.

WHAT IS A MORDANT IN THE CONTEXT OF NATURAL DYEING?

A mordant binds with a dye to make an insoluble compound and becomes part of the chemical bond between the dye and textile. This is key to being able to overdye and wash a textile without having the color wash away. If the mordant has been applied to the textile first, then the dye penetrates the fiber and attaches to the mordant, making an insoluble bond *within* the fiber.

When dyeing textiles, the mordant and dye are not usually placed in a single bath together like we did in Arizona, since some of the mordant and dye will bind together in the bath and will not be available to bind to the textile. Yet the savings of time, water, and fuel make this the preferred way of working in some parts of the world.

Sometimes a dye and mordant are intentionally bound together outside of a textile. The resultant insoluble compound is no longer a soluble dye but is transformed into a pigment, otherwise known as a dye lake. Lakes made from madder, lac, and cochineal have been important sources of pigment paints for artists through history.

SOURCES OF MORDANTS

Historically, mordant minerals were mined from the earth. Now, mordants are mostly manufactured, assuring their purity and lack of contaminants. Iron and copper can also be leached from iron or copper vessels or pieces of metal. This is most easily done when the bath is acidic. For instance, if wool is mordanted with alum (which is acidic) in an iron pot, the textile will absorb both alum and a small amount of iron. Similarly, if dyeing is done in an iron pot, then a small amount of iron will also be absorbed during the dye process.

Alum can also be extracted from bioaccumulating plants such as symplocos or camellia. The quantity of alum extracted depends on the presence of aluminum in the soil and in the acidity of the soil.

MORDANTS AND COLOR

The mordant also affects the color that is produced by the dye.

Alum is the most commonly used mordant. When bound to a dye, it results in the most brilliant clear yellows, reds, oranges, and pinks. When iron binds with a dye, the color deepens, darkens, or "saddens." Only a very small amount of iron is necessary to accomplish this. Iron can

The bond between mordant and dye is key to being able to wash a textile without the color washing away.

turn a yellow to an olive green or a pink to a purple. Small amounts also improve the lightfastness of any dye. Alum and iron are often used in combination: alum as a premordant (applied before the dyeing) and iron as a postmordant (applied after the dyeing) to tone the color.

The use of copper can move a yellow dye toward a greenish tone or slightly enhance a red dye, while also improving the lightfastness. Another metal used is tin, which can brighten and shift a cochineal dye from pink to scarlet.

Below: A rainbow of shades achieved by printing with several mordants (aluminum acetate, ferrous acetate, and titanium) and a single dye: pomegranate rind.

Photo courtesy of Homebody Textiles

A yarn that blends cellulose and protein fibers can be mordanted for either type, but the results may be very different. *From left:* An undyed 50% cotton/50% wool yarn; mordanted for cellulose with tannin and alum and dyed with madder root; and mordanted for protein and dyed with madder root.

> *Once a textile has been mordanted, it can be dyed immediately.*

Titanium is a mordant that Michel Garcia, natural dyer and researcher from France, has explored and introduced for mordant print applications. It also has uses in contact printing. When combined with a tannin, a golden orange color results.

Mordants are commonly referred to by the name of the metal. However, metals can appear in a variety of salts with different properties, which can cause confusion. For example, iron can refer to ferrous sulfate or ferrous acetate, both of which are used for different effects. Because the common name doesn't provide enough information, it's important to use the full chemical name.

MORDANTS AND FIBERS

Any discussion of the use of mordants goes hand in hand with understanding fiber types.

Protein fibers (wool and silk) make an electrical attachment to a mordant. There are a few dyes that attach to protein fibers without the use of a mordant. Some of these dyes (black walnut hulls, cochineal, cutch) will color the textile directly in long, slow dyebaths. Others (madder, rhubarb root, alkanet) can be used in combination with tannins and acids, and resemble the action of an acid dye.

Cellulose fibers (cotton, linen, hemp, etc.) do not make the same electrical attachment to a mordant. In fact, these do not make any ready attachment to the mordant. Instead, the mordant must be precipitated onto the textile. This can be done in one of two ways:

1. Apply a tannin, which has some affinity for the cellulose fiber. Then apply the mordant, which will bind to the tannin and thus to the textile.
2. A concentrated mordant can be precipitated onto a textile. This is often done using printing techniques such as block printing or silk screening. When the mordant is fully attached, then the textile can be dyed in an immersion bath.

Mordants for Dyeing

Common name	Chemical name(s)	Common use	Cautions
Alum	• Potassium aluminum sulfate • Aluminum sulfate • Ammonium alum (pickling alum)	The "bright" mordant: general premordant for all textiles.	Minimal*
Aluminum acetate	• Neutral aluminum triacetate • Dibasic aluminum acetate • Monobasic aluminum acetate	Mordant for cellulose immersion and for mordant printing.	Minimal
Iron	Ferrous sulfate	The "dark" mordant: tones color and increases lightfastness. Often used as a postmordant.	Minimal to the dyer and environment but can be damaging to silk
Iron	Ferrous acetate	Used in printing of cellulose and to tone colors on silk. Less damaging than ferrous sulfate.	Minimal
Tin	Stannous chloride	Will brighten cochineal.	Minimal (expensive)
Titanium	Potassium titanyl oxalate	The "golden" mordant: when combined with a tannin, a golden orange color will result. Used in mordant printing and contact printing to expand the palette.	Minimal, but dyes are less lightfast than those obtained with other mordants
Copper	Copper sulfate	Dulls colors and will increase lightfastness.	Not safe to dispose of in the ground or water system. Use only by leaching from a copper vessel or pipe.
Chrome	Potassium dichromate	Used a great deal in the past to extend the palette and increase lightfastness.	Not safe for use or disposal

*Minimal cautions: Do not ingest or breathe in. Always use designated cookware and utensils. It is best to wear gloves when handling. It is safe to dispose of solutions with plenty of water.

Once a textile has been mordanted, it can be dyed immediately. The textile can also be dried and stored indefinitely before dyeing.

MORDANTS AND DYE PLANT CATEGORIES

It is helpful to understand how mordants interact with the different categories of dye plants.

- *Flavonoids* are the source of most of our yellow dyes and include goldenrod, rabbitbrush, marigold, and weld. A flavonoid dye *always* requires a mordant on any fiber. Without the mordant, no dye will attach.

Indigo never requires a mordant.

- *Neoflavonoids,* found in logwood and brazilwood, always require a mordant on any fiber.
- *Anthraquinone dyes* are found in roots, barks, and insects (i.e., madder, rhubarb root, cochineal). They can be used with mordants or to dye protein fibers without the use of a mordant. A few of these will dye directly, but most will work best when combined with tannin and acid to aid in the attachment to the fiber. When dyeing cellulose, a mordant is always necessary.

WHAT IS NOT A MORDANT?

The term mordant is often used casually to describe any substance that will help a dye attach to a textile. In that context, it's easy to understand why these substances would be confused with mordants, but they do not bind with a dye to make an insoluble compound.

Soy milk, when made and used fresh, acts as an effective binder for pigment application on textiles. Soy is a protein substance and, in some cultures, has been used as a protein pretreatment on cellulose, instead of a tannin, in order to attach a mordant or even a dye. This often requires a long curing time.

Tannins (including tea, gallnut, sumac, etc.) are an integral part of mordanting cellulose, as noted above. They can also aid in the dyeing of protein fibers when a mordant is not used. But again, if there is no mordant, there is no insoluble compound. The presence of a tannin, either in the mordant or dye process, will always make a dye more lightfast.

Rhubarb leaves are a source of oxalic acid. Acids (oxalic acid, citric acid, or even white vinegar) can be used to increase the attachment of anthraquinone dyes to protein fibers when a mordant is not used. Oxalic acid and citric acid can also be used to remove mordants.

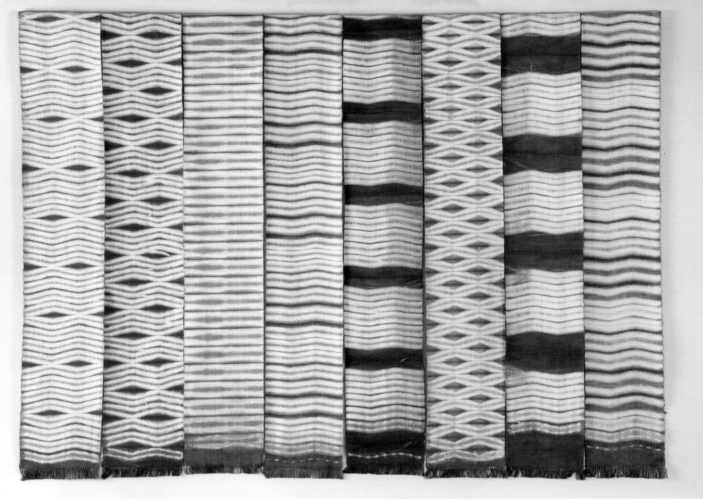

For the most brilliant greens, it is best to dye with the indigo first, then mordant, and finally apply the yellow dye. These cotton/linen pieces were dyed first with indigo and then with a variety of yellow dyes. If Indigo is dyed over the yellow dye, the mordant and dye can be damaged, and the color will not be as brilliant.

- *Tannins* are present in many plants and are sometimes used as dyes. Gallic tannins (from oak galls and sumac), although they can be used to assist in the mordanting or dyeing process, contain no dyes. Ellagic tannins (pomegranate and myrobalan) contain yellow colorants in addition to the tannin. Condensed tannins (quebracho and cutch) contain red colorants. Some tannins that contain colorants can be used to dye protein without the use of a mordant, but deeper color often results when a mordant is used. When dyeing cellulose, a mordant is always required.

- Indigo is an *indigoid* and never requires a mordant.

Above: Garden Series, Greens, Catharine Ellis, 2019. 35" x 45", cotton, linen, indigo, alum mordant, and various yellow dyes.

ARE MORDANTS TOXIC? DANGEROUS?

Joy was initially reluctant to explore natural dyeing with me. She lives and teaches in Denmark, where safety standards are very high, and she has always taught only the safest practices for both the artist's studio and industry. Joy perceived that many natural dyers were using mordants that were unsafe for studio use. Up to the early twentieth century when natural dyes were still being used in industry, lead, chrome, nickel, cobalt, and other metals were commonly added to expand the palette.

Once she determined that I wanted to do this as safely as possible and saw my notes from classes that I had taken with Michel Garcia, Joy was ready to help me navigate the topic of safe natural-dye practice.

The only mordants that I use regularly in my studio are alum and iron. Mabel Myers, my Navajo teacher, showed me how to identify the astringent nature of alum by tasting it. This is safe because aluminum sulfate (alum) is used in the making of pickles and in water treatment. I have also recently tested symplocos plants that grow in nearby South Carolina and are a good source of alum.

> *The only mordants that I use regularly in my studio are alum and iron.*

I use iron only in very small amounts (1%–2% of the fiber weight or less). Iron is in our blood, in the soil, and sometimes (sadly) in the water (which will always result in dull colors). Iron supplements are taken internally but dosages are very, very small because too much will result in iron poisoning. Conversely, large amounts of iron will damage a textile when it is exposed to ultraviolet light. Silk is especially vulnerable to damage from iron. Ferrous acetate is less corrosive to textiles than ferrous sulfate and is the only form of iron that is suitable for use on silk.

Copper is not safe to dispose of into the ground or water systems. For that reason, the only safe way to use this mordant is to leach the mineral from a copper vessel or pieces of copper pipe during the mordanting or dyeing process. The small amounts that are released from the metal will attach to the textile and thus not be disposed of as part of the bath.

Very occasionally, I use a small amount of tin with cochineal on wool to brighten the color. Sometimes I will use titanium, when printing, to extend the color palette.

I take general precautions with my mordants, using only designated pots and utensils for mordanting and dyeing. I wear gloves if I am immersing my hands. Dibasic and monobasic aluminum acetate are very light powders and easily become airborne. If you are sensitive, it's best to use a dust mask when measuring these mordants. Once they are in solution, mask wearing is not necessary.

Instead of printing or screening dyes onto cloth to create their designs, the artists at Homebody Textiles use screens to apply different mordants, then immerse the textiles in a dyebath for color effects.

Photo courtesy of Homebody Textiles

None of the mordants emit fumes when heated.

Good dyeing requires more than a knowledge of the dye plants and their sources. It also requires a thorough understanding of mordants, their use, and application. This is key to making good, long-lasting color on textiles.

tannin & iron

Kenya Miles

THERE ARE CERTAIN CHEMISTRIES in the natural world that are steeped in traditions with deep cultural knowledge and alchemy—where art and science converge. *Kapa* (or tapa) cloth of the Pacific, *bògòlanfini* of Mali, *kalamkari* of India, and *dorozome* of Japan are a few of the beautiful expressions of ancient techniques based on the chemistry between iron-rich earth and tannin-filled plants. Historically in North America, iron-and-tannin dyeing has its roots in indigenous groups' practices—leatherwork, quilling, basketry, and yarn dyeing. Distinctively regional, the process is achieved several ways: using iron-rich clay and a solution of rusted metal and vinegar or the naturally occurring mineral salt ferrous sulfate, activated by tannin from myriad regionally specific plants.

My personal journey printing with natural dyes and mordants began during a symposium at Maiwa in Vancouver, British Columbia. The four-day intensive led students from whole-cloth dyeing to thickening plant dyes and mordants, altering color by shifting pH, and discharging color using natural acids. It was there that I learned many of the recipes and techniques that have come to form the foundation of my textile practice.

Immediately following the symposium, I returned to my studio inspired and overwhelmed with the breadth of possibilities. Eagerly, I reviewed recipes and admired samples, but then a sort of paralysis set in. How can I apply these techniques, which often take days, to my process? How can my work be enriched by these practices? Unable to find a clear point of entry, I put away my notes, swatches, and newly acquired materials and found myself back in the safety of the indigo vat.

Many months on, the wedding of a dear friend was the occasion I needed to set out to explore and challenge my budding relationship with natural-dye printing. Inspired by the Tantric paintings of Rajasthan, I tried envisioning how to achieve that simple but elegant imagery using natural-dye techniques. For the foundation, I began by soaking a medium-weight hemp-and-silk fabric in myrobalan, which produces buttery yellow hues. Leaving the fabric in the bath overnight left a densely saturated gold luster on the silk thread.

The dark hues of iron-and-tannin painting or printing can add complexity to naturally dyed fabrics, like these pieces dyed first with indigo, brazilwood, and other dyestuffs.

Photo by Joe Coca

▶ Kapa cloth is made from the inner bark of the paper mulberry (*wauke*) that is cut, soaked, beaten, sometimes fermented, and laid to dry. Candlenut (*kukui*) is added using hand-carved bamboo stamps (*ohe kapala*) to produce deep reds and browns.

Wedding Tapa (Gatu Vakaviti). Republic of the Fiji Islands, twentieth century (M.2010.160). Inner bark of the paper mulberry plant.
Gift of Patricia Manney and Eric Gruendemann.

Courtesy of Los Angeles County Museum of Art

▼ *Kalamkari* is a multilayered process that begins by soaking white cotton in a concentrated paste of *harde* (my-robalan, the tannin-rich dried nuts of *Terminalia chebula*) thinned with water and buffalo milk. Designs are printed or sketched onto the fabric, later to be overpainted with an ink made using the water from boiled rice (*kanji*), rusted iron pieces, and river stones (*kittankul*). The reaction between the myrobalan-soaked fabric and the ink creates deep black outlines, which are often filled with rich pigments.

A kalamkari design.

Photo courtesy of Maiwa

Bògòlanfini is created using strips or bands of cotton cloth that are sewn together and soaked in a bath of tannin-rich plants such as *nglama*. Once the strips have dried, symbols are painted on the cloth with mud rich in iron. This process of painting the symbols over and over by layering tannin and iron deepens the shade from brown and gray to black (see page 82).

Photo by Joe Coca

▲ *Dorozome* is a fiber-dyeing process created by macerating and boiling the wood from the Japanese hawthorn (*sharinbai*) tree. Along with an alkaline substance, white cotton fabric is soaked in a bath of the dye solution. Once dried, the fiber is soaked in local river mud.

These traditional *dorozome* textiles bear labels that state their origin—and offer a sketch of the manufacturing process on the brown label.
Textile courtesy of John Marshall.

After several tries to achieve rich black colors on silk through vat-dyeing with tannin that produced only deep brown, I added ferrous sulfate directly to the bath (in small amounts, as iron is corrosive to fiber) and pushed the color to gray. Seeing this made me realize I could push even further. Once it dried, I added a concentration of myrobalan dye and water to the cloth. I then made a thickened dye paste of iron and vinegar that I brushed directly onto the silk cloth. Almost immediately, the color that was a pale gray deepened to a delicious vine black. And just like that, I was hooked!

It was as if I had uncovered a portal to some cosmic wisdom. From that point on, I studied and practiced various applications of iron and tannin, using materials local to me (then in Northern California) such as oak gall and black walnut. I experimented with various ways of applying thickened tannin and iron using silk screens, sponges, brushes, and stamps. Years of practice have pushed me to think about simple, accessible ways to achieve the vibrant reaction between iron-rich earth and tannin-rich plants. Translating these techniques and practices into modern Western craft can offer an exciting lens into our contemporary life while taking on new relevant pathways.

We are no longer required to grow, mine, forage, and harvest for natural materials, but we still must sit with these natural elements even after they are unpackaged from the ready supplier. How can we collaborate with these earthly materials? What will come of any combination of these elements?

What new discoveries will we make along the way?

BASIC IRON-AND-TANNIN DYEING METHOD

Here is a general step-by-step process for working with iron and tannin. For formulas using a variety of tannin-rich plants, *The Maiwa Guide to Natural Dyes* is an excellent source of recipes.

Depending on the background color of the textile (i.e., fabric dyed with indigo), I may add

Painting with iron on a tannin-soaked fabric can give a reddish, rusty look, but immersing the piece in a tannin bath turns the red to dark gray.

Photos by Kenya Miles

Soaking cotton fabric overnight in a tannin solution creates a tan color and prepares the surface for painting with iron. The iron paste should be thick enough to be used with a brush or stamp to leave a crisp design.

iron as the first layer, then lay tannin on top. Other times, I begin with a fabric mordanted in tannin and paint iron on top. If I want to enrich the color further, I may add tannin once more to the design.

Equipment

- Immersion blender or whisk
- Padded working surface
- Brushes or stamps
- Jar
- Nylon produce bag
- Iron
- Burner or stove
- Enamel or stainless steel pot

Materials

- Natural-fiber cloth, scoured well to re-move sizing, waxes, and finishes
- Tannin-rich plant matter (myrobalan, oak gall, black walnut, etc.)
- Distilled white vinegar
- Ferrous sulfate
- Calcium hydroxide (pickling lime)
- Thickener (gum arabic, guar gum, gum tragacanth)
- Wheat bran and/or calcium carbonate (ground chalk)

Fabric Preparation

1. Break down any whole tannin materials with a mallet so that the pieces are split apart. Place any large pieces or chunks in a fine net produce bag.
2. Add powdered or bagged tannin to the water and bring to a simmer for 30–45 minutes. (When creating the mixture, I go by look and feel. If you prefer to measure the materials, the weight of the tannin should be 10%–35% of the weight of the fabric, depending on the depth of shade you want to achieve.)

3. Add fabric to dyebath. Simmer on low for 30–45 minutes.

4. Remove fabric from the bath and allow it to dry or sit overnight.

IRON PASTE

(**Note:** *Always wear a mask and gloves when working with powders and mineral salts.*)

1. Add vinegar to a jar.

2. Add ferrous sulfate.

3. Add calcium hydroxide to the jar.

4. Blend all ingredients together. This is easiest with an immersion blender, but it can be done with a whisk.

5. Add thickener and blend. (I have found that iron solution is less stable in cooler temperatures and requires more thickener; in warmer months, smaller amounts of thickener work best and will also expand as the mixture sits.) It's a gentle balance between soup and gelatin. If the paste is too thick, it will sit on the surface and not penetrate the fabric. If it's too thin, the paste will spread on the fabric, creating blurred imagery.

Fabric Painting

1. Lay tannin-infused fabric flat, remove wrinkles or creases with the iron, and pin or stretch onto a padded surface.

2. Paint or print as desired on your fabric. Browns, grays, and blacks will appear as the paste dries. Different tannins produce different hues; this is something to experiment with. Adding additional washes of tannin over the iron once set will darken shades.

Setting the Dye

1. Leave the fabric to dry out of direct sunlight.

2. To preserve your imagery (and not have your hard work go to waste), you must set or neutralize the chemical reaction on your fabric in a bath of warm water and calcium carbonate or wheat bran. Take care to stir the calcium carbonate in well. You can bag the wheat bran in a nylon produce bag to prevent it from collecting on your fabric.

AN IRON OPTION

In place of vinegar and ferrous sulfate, make an iron solution using scrap iron covered with 1 part water, 1 part distilled white vinegar. Leave the covered jar in a dry, dark place for a week or longer to form a slurry. Strain out the metal and use the mixture. This will require some testing, as the amount of iron is unknown. You can test the strength of the iron solution by dipping a paintbrush in the mix and brushing it on vegetable-tanned leather or fabric mordanted in tannin (see page 39).

Photo by Kenya Miles

Photo by Adriaan Louw, *True Colors* (Thrums Books)

delicious darkness

Keith Recker

Dark silt from the river is left to ferment, yielding a smooth slip.

WHEN TANNINS AND IRON-RICH MUD combine, storied blacks and browns are born. Some textile historians have hypothesized that a combination of plant tannins and iron-rich mud may have been mastered quite early on by our ancestors. Fishnets made dramatically dark by repeated drags along a muddy riverbank may have been the first clue. However ancient its origins, though, mudcloth is still very much alive in the twenty-first century, serving up deep blacks and dark browns that intrigue the eye.

WHERE ART MEETS MUD

In Mali, mudcloth is called *bògòlanfini,* a joining of the Bambara words for "mud," "made with," and "cloth." The process starts with

dark, iron-rich silt dredged from the Niger River or from mucky pond bottoms. The dark silt is decanted into large clay vessels, covered in a layer of water, and left alone for a year to ferment. What's left at the end of the fermenting and settling process is a smooth liquid-clay slip that handles a bit like paint.

Before the advent of imported machine-made cloth, the process began with soft, lofty African fabric, handspun from cotton and woven in strips about as wide as a hand that are sewn together to create blankets or panels for clothing. Strip-woven cotton is still used sometimes, though lately something akin to light cotton duck is usually the base. Cotton must be soaked in a tannin-rich bath in order for the mud to do its dyeing work. The leaves of the *nglama* tree, a type of African birch, are the most common source of tannin at this stage, though other leaves and barks can come into play; the nglama vat imparts a bright ochre-yellow color to the cloth.

Traditionally, artisans then trace ancient ideograms onto the bright yellow cloth, recalling a time almost out of memory when a bògòlanfini garment telegraphed messages about its wearer. A double line of opposing zigzags means "the brave man's belt." A single tooth-like line of connected triangles means "the jealous husband's teeth." An hourglass shape represents the drum used to call warriors to battle. Women wore mudcloth, too, and some ideograms recall traditionally feminine ideals. A dot within a circle describes a traditional round house and the family living within it. A group of four circumflexes declares the wearer to be a woman of leisure. In mudcloth from the area around Bamako, these ideograms appeared in white against a dark mud-dyed background, requiring a bògòlanfini maker to meticulously brush mud all over the background of the cloth, avoiding the geometric shapes of the ideograms. As many as four coats of mud were required to create deep black tones. In some rural communities, browns were prized over blacks because brown provided better camouflage for hunters. This meant more layers of nglama and other tannin-based colorants and less coverage with mud. Once the tinting and washing process was complete, the ideograms were whitened by brushing them with mild bleaching agents.

In the mid 1970s in Bamako, Mali, all the varia-

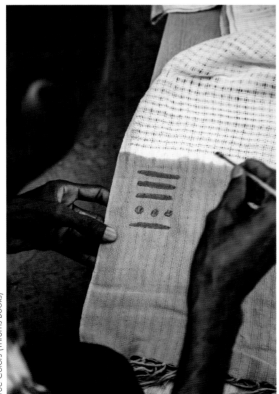

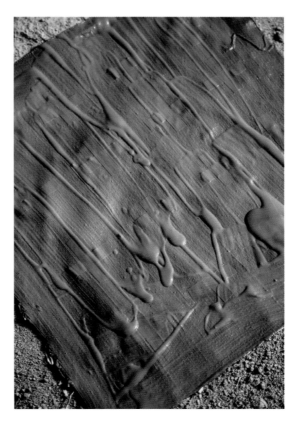

Far left: A painted design on mordanted cloth.

Left: The iron-rich slip is painted thickly onto the mordanted cloth.

Photos by David Crookes (Courtesy of Design Network Africa and Trevyn McGowan), *True Colors* (Thrums Books)

Boubacar Doumbia

and yellows of nglama, and the white of cotton have been joined by indigo blues, olive greens, and a host of other colors. Traditional ideograms still appear, but often in a context of freehand geometry and figural elements according to the vision of each artist. "Bògòlanfini carries a message for our community in design form. We extend that message in very contemporary ways using the technique," comments Boubacar.

Many young people have embraced the technique for its artistic potential, communal identity, and economic benefit. Boubacar has taught many of them at his nonprofit center, Ndomo, in the small city of Ségou, located along the Niger River between Bamako and Mopti.

OF YAMS AND MUD

Across the world in China, the tradition of gambiered silk channels the power of plant tannins and river mud into different results. Dating back at least to the fifteenth-century Ming dynasty, and possibly a millennium before that, the dark, mineral-heavy mud of Guangdong province's river deltas was used to make a silk prized for its unique color, texture, and drape.

The tannin in this process comes from a yam, *Dioscorea cirrhosa*, which is used in traditional Chinese medicine for its antibacterial and antiviral properties. It is also said to moderate humidity, which according to traditional Chinese medicine is bad for the body.

The making of gambiered silk, which also goes by tea silk, mud silk, and other names, is governed by the seasons. From April to Novem-

tions of mudcloth blossomed into something new. Six art students, impatient with their school's Eurocentric curriculum, formed *Groupe Kasobane*. Mudcloth was their chosen medium, and they used the traditional combination of plant-based tannins and iron-rich mud in new ways.

As Boubacar Doumbia, one of Kasobane's founders, says, "We were the pioneers who explored mudcloth as a means of expression in the form of contemporary art." In their hands, mudcloth expanded from a language of geometric symbols into expressive scenes of nature and village life. It became a form of painting.

Thanks to influencers such as the Kasobane pioneers, creativity around mudcloth has exploded in Mali, with tourists and international buyers as principal markets. The black of mud, the browns ber, yards of silk are soaked in vats of diluted fermenting yam juice. The greater the number of soaks, the deeper and more gorgeous the resulting orange-brown color. Some makers immerse and dry the silk up to 40 times.

Once the yam portion of the process is complete, the silk is rolled out onto fields or riverbanks to receive a slathered coating of iron-rich mud, much like bògòlanfini. The side facing down remains orange-brown, while the top side takes on the lustrous black of the mud, often with subtle undulations of color and finish absorbed from the inevitably uneven coating of mud. After laundering and pressing, no two batches (or even yards) are ever exactly alike. The mineral content and thickness of the mud can vary, pollution in the water can shift the shade of color, and the strength of the sunlight curing the fabric can create nuances as well. The silk is sometimes described as papyrus-like and sometimes as behaving like thin leather. Thanks to the properties of the textile, clothes made from it have a gorgeous drape and volume, which is said to improve across a lifetime of wearing.

Liang Zhu, a resident of Shunde in Guangdong and manager of one of the very few extant gambiered silk ateliers pursuing traditional methods, says, "I live at the mercy of the weather." Yams and mud must be on the fresh side. Rain is not helpful, and sun needs to be plentiful. "It usually takes a week to finish a 20-meter piece of silk," Liang says, reminding us that time is also an ingredient in a process that involves so many repeated steps to build up color and finish. In 2019, Marcella Echavarria, photographer, author, editor, and sustainable development

Photos courtesy of Marcella Echavarria

consultant, created a line of gambiered silk clothing called Noir Handmade. The forms are simple. The patterns come from playing with the black and brown surfaces of the fabric and interspersing bits of silks dyed in other colors.

Marcella has created four collections so far, not adhering to any sort of fashion calendar. She offers the clothing only once in a while, seasons and weather and inspiration permitting. Modern wearers treasure the clothing for some of the same reasons gambiered silk has always been valued: it remains light and airy even in hot weather. "The Chinese call it 'perfumed cloud clothing,'" Marcella says, clearly in love with the poetry of the phrase as well as the quality of the cloth.

Top: Silk mordanted with fermented yam juice is rolled out and coated with mud, giving the rich black color of iron-and-tannin dyeing.

Above: Marcella Echavarria's line of gambiered silk clothing, Noir Handmade, celebrates the richness of this traditional cloth.

keeping traditions alive

Linda Ligon

IT HOLDS A PLACE OF PRIDE ON A SHELF
in my office: an unassuming framed piece,
about 9 by 11 inches, holding the beginnings of
a tiny four-selvedge rug woven with handspun
wool, dyed in seven different colors from plants
native to the Navajo Nation. A family member
found it in a little shop somewhere in Okla-
homa, but its home of origin was New Mexico,
south of Gallup near the tiny community of
Pine Springs.

That's where the family of Mabel Burnside
Myers has continued to produce these cultural treasures: spinning the yarn, gathering
the plants, dyeing, labeling, weaving. It's not a
trivial undertaking. They're continuing a project begun by their mother, their grandmother,
some 70 years ago.

Her life had been remarkable. Born in 1922
and graduated from high school in 1938,

RED ONION SKI
Tł'ochin łich

ROSEHIPS
Chọọh

SMALL SNAKEWE
Ch'ildiilyési

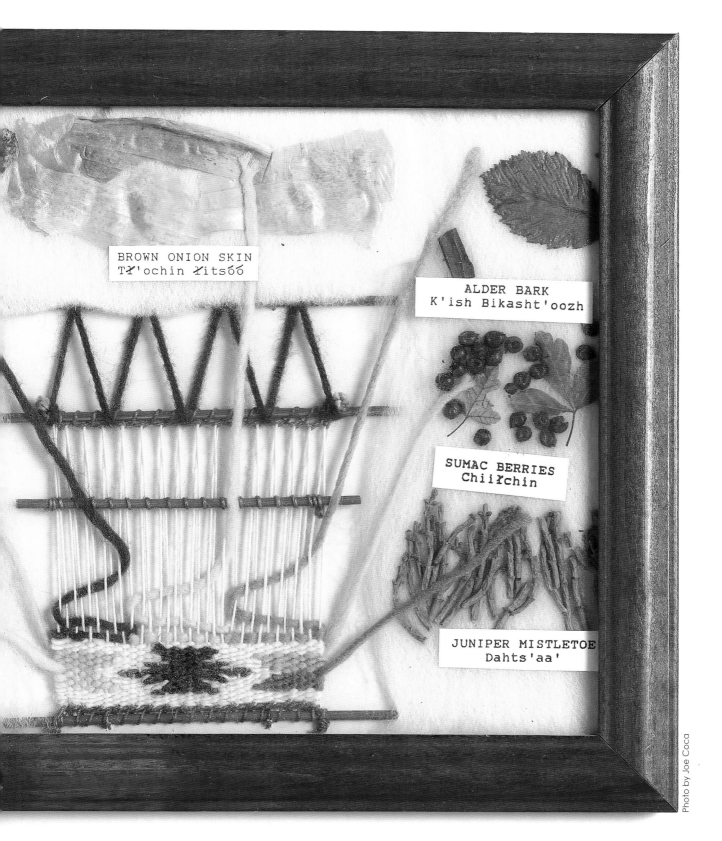

BROWN ONION SKIN
Tłʼochin Łitsóó

ALDER BARK
Kʼish Bikashtʼoozh

SUMAC BERRIES
Chiiłchin

JUNIPER MISTLETOE
Dahtsʼaaʼ

A portrait of Mabel Burnside Myers as a young woman with one of her prize-winning rugs.

Photo by Don Dedera, published here with permission of the Dedera family

1958. In her soft-spoken way, she affirmed that being home with family and weaving were more important than the generous salary she had received working in Shiprock. She shows a rug, a masterpiece, that she had woven using 85 natural-dyed colors.

This mastery of such a wide range of dye colors somehow led to the idea of presenting them in a unique format, attractive to collectors and museums and tourists. Creating the framed charts became a little cottage industry for her family. Her children and grandchildren have memories of driving along the remote roads of the Navajo Nation, collecting leaves and twigs and berries along the way and then watching the colors emerge in the boiling vats in their hogan.

Mabel's daughter, Isabel Deschinny, began to learn the dyes from her mother when she was only ten, and she has led the project since her mother's passing in 1978. In fact, her framed chart featuring 87 colors took overall Best of Show at the Navajo Nation Fine Arts Fair in 2019. It's a majestic 3 feet by 6 feet, with an exquisite miniature rug at its heart.

Mabel Burnside was head of the weaving department at the tribal vocational school in Shiprock before she was thirty. She had participated in the beginnings of a natural-dye book at Fort Wingate Vocational High School much earlier than that; she's remembered as carrying sample cards wrapped in dyed yarn to serve as reference as she taught the skills. This was just a couple of years after high school.

Pine Springs and her family—which included five children—called her home, though. We see her weaving in her hogan in a National Educational Television documentary film (*The Navajo [Part I]: The Search for America*) made in

My little piece, some colors faded with age, must be one of many hundreds, or even thousands, produced by Mabel Burnside Myers and the Deschinny family. You can find charts of all sizes and complexity in galleries and on eBay, selling for many hundreds of dollars. They are all true to the original: carefully warped little four-selvedge rugs, neatly typed plant labels in English and Navajo, alive with the colors of the land.

COLORS FROM THE LAND

Mabel Burnside Myers was not alone in her efforts to record the use of native plants in Navajo weaving. The Home Economics Department at the Fort Wingate Vocational High School felt a commitment to publishing information that would be useful to people from all parts of the Navajo Nation. Beginning in 1934, Mrs. Nonabah G. Bryan, who was teaching weaving, began the project of experimenting with native plants and creating usable dye recipes. This resulted first in a mimeographed bulletin produced by the school, and later a booklet published by the Bureau of Indian Affairs. This booklet, *Navajo Native Dyes: Their Preparation and Use*, includes plant illustrations by Charles Keetsie Shirley and delves into the uses of 35 plants and minerals.

Beginning in 1974, William Rieske of Historic Indian Publishers in Salt Lake City acquired two framed pieces created by Mabel Burnside Myers's family and cross-referenced their dyed samples with the Bryan book. **Here's a short list . . .**

Blue-flowered lupine *(Lupinus kingii)*

Illustration by Charles Keetsie Shirley

Common name	Genus and species	Color	Parts used
Blue-flowered lupine	*Lupinus kingii*	greenish yellow	flowers, leaves, stems
Cactus, prickly pear	*Opuntia polyacantha*	rose	fresh fruits
Canaigre	*Rumex hymenosepalus*	medium brown	dried roots
Cliff rose	*Cowania stansburiana*	gold	twigs and leaves
Gambel oak	*Quercus gambelii*	dulled tan	bark
Ground lichen	*Parmelia mollusca*	light orange	whole plant
Indian paintbrush	*Castilleja integra*	tan	blossoms
Juniper, one seeded	*Juniperus monosperma*	orange-tan	bast and twigs
Mountain mahogany	*Cercocarpus montanus*	soft reddish brown	root bark
Navajo tea	*Thelesperma gracile*	orange	leaves, stems, flowers
Purple larkspur	*Delphinium scaposum*	greenish gray	petals
Rabbitbrush	*Chrysothamnus latisqualis*	bright yellow	blossoms and twigs
Russian thistle	*Salsola kali*	rich olive	leaves and twigs
Sumac, three-leaved	*Rhus trilobata*	light orange-brown	ripe berries
Wild privet (ironwood)	*Forestiera neomexicana*	light gray	berries
Wild rubber plant	*Hymenoxys metcalfei*	bright yellow	leaves, stems, flowers
Yellow beeplant	*Cleome serrulata*	yellow-green	whole plant

AJRAKH ARTIST
Sufiyan Khatri

Mary Anne Wise

SUFIYAN AWAKES TO SOUNDS OF RAIN. *The steady rooftop patter signals that today will not be a good day to dye. The sound means the monsoon rains have come and cloth will not dry in this weather. Still, the sound makes him happy. He is not alone: throughout the dry, semiarid region of the Kutch, in the western state of Gujurat, India, everyone celebrates.*

The region's dusty and barren countryside will soon transform into beautiful lush and green landscapes. Before this monsoon season ends, inshallah *(God willing), water tables will be replenished to levels not seen in seven years.*

Today may not be a good day to dye, but it's a good day to be in the workshop. A good day to repair the broken table leg and build a new shelf to contain his ever-expanding array of wooden blocks for printing. He approaches these tasks with confidence. Growing up, Sufiyan's grandfather insisted he learn how systems work: from repairing his own bicycle, to carving the wooden blocks used in their printing process, to repairing the workshop's plumbing. At thirty-seven years old, Sufiyan, a tenth-generation block printer, possesses the self-sufficiency born to those who rely upon their hands to sustain their livelihood.

With the chores completed, he looks forward to his design time. Tea in hand, he settles at one of his empty 8-meter-long tables. The tables are built to accommodate the printing of saris, allowing the length of fabric to stretch across the table's long expanse. Printing comes to a halt during the monsoons, and so instead, Sufiyan sits down and reflects upon the changes brought by the rains. He anticipates flamingos, Gujurat's state bird, returning to the region, perhaps soon to alight upon the seasonal marshes adjacent to the nearby Rann desert. Flamingos arrive from Siberia to nest in the Kutch, and the memory of standing on the marsh's edge in years past to observe these elegant birds inspires. He appreciates the significance of combining the flamingo design with ajrakh: *both were nearly lost, and both have returned to the Kutch.*

Opposite, top: Sufiyan Khatri pulls a printed textile from the indigo vat. *Below left:* Block printing requires great precision. *Below right:* Hand-carved wooden printing blocks from the family collection.

Photos by Flo Hanatschek unless otherwise indicated

"Ajrakh" is derived from the Arabic word meaning blue—but the word also describes the ancient and complex natural print and dye process found in Pakistan and also just across the border in India's Kutch. The process involves up to 16 steps completed over a 14- to 21-day period. Experienced ajrakh practitioners expand upon the interpretation and give more meaning to the word, saying "keep it today." This phrase may be interpreted to remind those learning the printing techniques to "stay in the moment with this process, do not hurry along, for the best results cannot be rushed. Let the fabric dry and rest in the hot sun; you will get a better print and a better dye, too."

Fabrics that have been printed and dyed are laid out in the yard to dry.

ally correct symmetrical designs suggestive of harmony and balance. The hand-carved wooden-block designs are informed by geometric shapes, flower and leaf patterns, elements from Moghul architecture, and Iranian and Islamic influences, too.

Factory-made textiles arrived in the Kutch in the 1950s, and this introduction undermined local ajrakh production. To compete with the factory textiles, many traditional ajrakh artisans switched to synthetic dyes, and the use of natural dyes disappeared. In 1970, Sufiyan's grandfather, Mohammed Sidiq, a renowned block printer who, like everyone else in the region, used synthetic dyes, received a request for natural-dyed yardage. Curious about the near-lost process, he began experimenting. He was an engaged learner— even when there were no orders for natural-dyed fabrics, he wanted to understand the nuances of pairing a specific fiber with a specific natural dye. Through the use of natural dyes, he developed a deep understanding of the world around him along with a passionate commitment to preserving traditional ajrakh dye and print processes as an important cultural legacy. Today, Mohammed Sidiq is widely recognized for reintroducing natural dyes to the Kutch; he taught his three sons, who taught their sons, including Sufiyan and his brother Junaid. Sufiyan is now teaching his son.

Traditional ajrakh colors signify the universe: red is for the earth, black is for darkness, white is for clouds, and blue embraces the entire universe. Historically, ajrakh designs were created from a specified set of 24 hand-carved wooden blocks. Traditional ajrakh printers cover the entire fabric in block pattern grids that seamlessly dovetail to form pleasing and proportion-

In the mid-1970s, urban markets rediscovered traditional ajrakh and kindled a demand. Soon other workshops in the Kutch began using natural dyes, too. Increased demand attracted attention from India's National Institute of Design, who asked for a wider color palette, and over time, more colors from other natural-dye substances evolved. The ajrakh palette now includes yellows, greens, browns, and purples. To achieve these colors, Sufiyan uses the same plant, mineral, and insect sources as his father. He purchases his supplies from his grandfather's same local source. His potpourri of ingredients to print and dye the colors includes lac (an insect excretion) and plant ingredients such as indigo, rhubarb root, tamarisk flower, pomegranate, turmeric, onion skins, logwood, madder root and plant, gum arabic, and *dhavdi* flower. To "fix" the color, that is, to create a chemical bond between the fabric and the natural dye and hold the color fast, he uses alum as a mordant. Myrobalan, a tannin derived from the *Terminalia chebula* tree, is used to bring out the richness of the dye colors, especially reds and blacks. Henna, clay, and lime play roles, along with adjusting the levels of acidity or alkalinity of the water with the mineral sources mentioned and making thick pastes with these materials to resist the dyes.

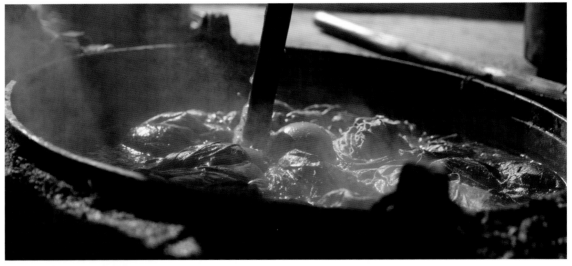

Photo by Joe Coca

FOCUSING ON THE COMBINATION *of the flamingo with ajrakh prints, Sufiyan draws several flamingos, varying the scale each time. Finally, he selects the larger drawing because the size aligns with how the stole (scarf) falls across the back and shoulders. Sufiyan remembers his first attempt at a flamingo design, a design for which he used* Kariyano, *a resist paste thickened with lime and acacia tree gum painted on the fabric that is then submerged in an indigo bath. He reflects how the recipe for this paste has not changed*

Above: Flamingo stole of mulberry silk with traditional ajrakh colors. The stole was first washed in soda ash to remove the starch, then soaked in a tannic myrobalan solution. It was first printed with fermented iron for the black outlines, then printed with indigo for the blue areas, then printed in alum, and finally boiled in madder for the red.

Opposite: A bubbling fermented iron dyebath and fermentation residue from the indigo vat.

his grandfather taught him the technique. *Despite multiple attempts, the painted resist lines were not crisp and the design was difficult to read. And so, instead, he thought of creating the flamingo design in stitched shibori, a resist technique that offers more precision.*

Having decided upon the flamingo's scale, he turns his attention to choosing the correct scale of blocks to decorate the pallu *(end of the stole that drapes over the shoulder). His decision to combine flamingos with traditional ajrakh, both symbols of resurgence, means his palette is predetermined: he will print patterns in rust reds and blues with faint black outlines. He makes a mental note to check his dye powders to determine their age, for the strongest colors are from dyes less than four months old. He will need fermented iron for the black outlines, indigo for the area surrounding the flamingo,*

Above left: This handwoven *dupatta* (shawl), handspun with pashmina, is printed with a traditional pattern in a contemporary color palette. The dupatta was first washed in soda ash, then soaked in a tannic myrobalan solution to enrich natural dye colors. It was printed with a resist paste of lime and gum arabic for the white outline; the second printing was indigo and the third was alum. The dupatta was then dyed with iron, washed, and boiled with tamarisk flower. *Above right:* A silk dupatta of traditional design with historic ajrakh colors. After preparation with soda ash and myrobalan solution, it was printed with a resist paste of lime and gum arabic for the white outline; the second printing was indigo; the third printing was iron; then it was painted with alum and washed and boiled with alizarin and tamarisk flower.

and madder for the rust reds in the pallu.

After printing the pallus, he takes the flamingo drawing and the stole to his friend Yakub, a shibori artist who lives nearby. Yakub interprets Sufiyan's design, drawing it onto the stole, and then he gives it to one of the 20 women who stitch his shibori. She loads her needle with a fine thread and traces the line drawing using stitches so tight they will resist Sufiyan's dyes. Back in his workshop, Sufiyan dips the stitched stole into the indigo bath repeatedly until he achieves a deep and mellow midnight blue. Then he removes the stole from the bath and begins to rinse and rinse and rinse until the water runs clear. Holding his breath, he removes the stitches to reveal the flamingo design and once removed, "Dhaj che!" (wow). He is pleased.

Collaborating with others may not have occurred

Above left: A gaji silk dupatta of traditional design with colors introduced within the past 40 years. After the usual preparatory steps, it was printed with lime and gum arabic for the lighter outlines. The second printing was with fermented iron rust, the third with clay mixed with alum. Then it was dyed with indigo, washed, boiled with tamarisk flower, then dyed with alum, washed again, and finally boiled with pomegranate and turmeric for the green areas. *Above right:* This shawl is printed on handspun, handwoven 500-count cotton khadi cloth with an extremely intricate pattern requiring a high degree of skill to print. The lighter outlines were printed with a resist paste of lime and gum arabic; the second printing was with clay and alum; the third printing was with clay, alum, and alizarin; then it was dyed with indigo, washed, and boiled with tamarisk flower.

to Sufiyan but for a 2007 chance encounter with British designer Simon Marks. Simon had worked with a different block printer to achieve a particular design, but the design didn't work and the desired effect fell flat. Looking for a new block printer to interpret his pattern, Simon approached Sufiyan, who studied the block's design and determined what went wrong and how to fix it. Revisions were made, and to Simon's delight, the print succeeded. The two developed a respectful rapport and continued their collaboration. Sufiyan was excited to work with Simon; successfully achieving Simon's design objectives felt satisfy-

ing. But in the process, along the way, Sufiyan's own design ideas surfaced. He found himself approaching traditional ajrakh printing with a sense of curiosity and a desire to explore the possibilities as his inherited and ancient aesthetic intersected with other sources. He began to consider the tensions between positive and negative space and how to create perspective along with an awareness of foreground and background. Traditional ajrakh designs are relatively flat; learning to "see" the dimensional quality of printed patterns changed his vision and expanded his realm of possibilities. More opportunities for collaboration followed:

he spent time working with a designer from Amsterdam and another artist from Japan, Shiori Mukkai. Shiori came for a week and stayed for two years, interning and innovating her design sensibilities alongside Sufiyan's traditional knowledge. Soon other Japanese visitors learned of Sufiyan's workshop and came to visit, including Fumie Kobayashi. In 2017, Fumie arranged for Sufiyan to travel to Japan on a cultural exchange program during which he participated in workshops and trade shows and absorbed Japanese culture. Speaking of his Japanese colleagues, Sufiyan grows animated, saying, "I feel a kinship with the Japanese. We have the same 50-year earthquake cycle, and this changes our water tables. It actually changes the [pH of the] water, and we have to learn again to adjust our dye recipes." He admires the Japanese aesthetics of simplicity and clarity of design, and he envisions this influence will continue to inform his work. In addition to growing an appreciation for the aesthetics of his host, Sufiyan learned the method of indigo fermentation known as *sukomo*, which achieves some of the best indigo colors he has ever used.

It's not only the Japanese with whom he has a kinship. Like artists and craftspeople around the globe, Sufiyan finds meaning and makes his way through adversity by practicing his craft. *Inshallah.*

Opposite: Sufiyan Ismail Khatri carries on his family's traditions with great care in his workshop in Ajrakhpur, Kutch, Gujarat, India. *Below:* Indigo is a critical element in many of his fabrics.

Shakil's batik

BRINGING BACK TRADITION

Satish Reddy

TUCKED AWAY IN A REMOTE VILLAGE of Mundra, a port city on the Gulf of Kutch in the district of Gujarat, India, Shakil Khatri's family has been practicing the craft of batik block printing for at least six generations.

Before the 1950s, when petroleum-based paraffin was introduced, the patterns of traditional batik used the oil of the pilu tree (*Salvadora persica*), locally known as *kakhan,* as a resist. It has a very thick consistency but is sensitive to heat—so much so that block printing with pilu oil was carried out only in the cool early-morning hours.

The fabric printed with pilu oil was dyed in cold vats of indigo or fermented iron for shades of blue and black, respectively. Then the iron-dyed fabrics, washed and free from pilu oil, were boiled in madder to get red tones in the previously white-resisted areas. The overdye of red didn't affect the black background, and this color combination of red and black was very common in traditional batik. These natural-dyed batik fabrics were not traded beyond the local farming communities of the Ahir, Baniya, and Patel castes.

By the time Shakil Khatri embarked upon his journey with batik in 2002, the traditional ways of making and trading had all but disappeared. The consumer shift happened in the late 1940s, the post-independence period, as factory-made textiles found their way into the local markets. Their enticing variety lured the locals away from handmade textiles.

This shift prompted many batik artisans to leave the craft. Shakil's granduncle Ismail, a well-educated gentleman, left for Mumbai to earn a livelihood. The craft's artisans were in vigorous search of new markets.

In Bombay, Ismail saw batik textiles from other parts of India. They were resisted with paraf-

fin wax and dyed in cold-water naphthol-based dyes. Emulating the new market conditions, Kutch batik transitioned from natural dyes to naphthol-based dyes. The new batik prints were modern and bright and colorful.

This revived batik. But this moment of sudden change proved to be a bleak period as the craft and the maker lost their identities and the prestige they had once enjoyed. The market began to be saturated with low-priced, poorly done batik textiles.

"It was the 1990s. As the batik crisis deepened, my father, Kasam, and his brothers Mohammed and Ayub felt the need for new alternatives to emerge in order to sustain life in batik,"

Fabrics block printed with wax are ready for dyeing in Shakil's workshop.

All photos by Jody Slocum

The productivity of Shakil's workshop is impressive, given the exacting nature of the process.

says Shakil. Kasam, a master printer and block designer, innovated with prints and designs. His brothers Mohammed and Ayub focused on the quality of dye and color. Soon their workshop began to produce textiles of high workmanship. Though unquestionably good, the textiles still lacked the authenticity of the past—the identity and the prestige those textiles had borne. Or so thought Shakil's uncle Ayub when he set about the revival of batik with natural dyes in 2005. Meanwhile Shakil developed a fine, delicate hand for printing textiles of exquisite beauty.

Ayub convinced Shakil to enter the design program at Kala Raksha Vidhyalaya, an art school program that imparts design education to Kutch artisans and builds networks. Shakil began the course in 2009 in order to experience design and social interactions that went beyond consumer capitalism. "The interactions there with designers, craft activists, and educators made me realize the oblivion the craft has sunk into. People weren't even aware of the existence of batik in Kutch," Shakil says. Faced with this vulnerable situation, Shakil understood the need to change the approach to his craft and

Shakil's father, Kasam, amassed a large library of hand-carved printing blocks over three decades.

> *"Working with natural dyes in batik is a very delicate process because of the presence of wax. It takes one week to prepare batik textiles in natural dyes, while it takes only a day with chemical dyes,"* says Shakil. *But the resulting natural tones in batik are very unusual compared to other natural-dyed textiles. They are pastel in shade. Calm and muted. Simple and elegant.*

to fashion batik, making textiles that would be more durable in the message they carry.

Judy Frater, director and founder of Kala Raksha, noticed the fine craftsmanship of Shakil's textiles. She helped him foster collaborations with designers and encouraged him to pursue the use of natural dyes. Shakil, too, understood the challenge of making fashion sustainable. But going back to the roots and working with natural dyes meant reorchestrating the pace of the craft.

"It was only my uncle Ayub's passing away in 2013 that made me pause and acknowledge his vision and think of the social nature of fashion.

That the sociality of fashion and creating identities is also about the stories we want to tell about the craft," adds Shakil. "I took up the revival from where my uncle left off. He achieved success with indigo but was very limited with other natural dyes. Indigo is a cold-dye vat. But other natural dyes require long application of heat for the dye to adhere to the cloth, which affects the areas resisted with paraffin wax."

A weeklong natural-dye workshop at Kala Raksha helped Shakil to understand the behavior of natural dyes at different temperatures. "Working with natural dyes in batik is a very delicate process because of the presence of wax. It takes one week to prepare batik textiles in natural dyes, while it takes only a day with chemical dyes," says Shakil. But the resulting natural tones in batik are very unusual compared to other natural-dyed textiles. They are pastel in shade. Calm and muted. Simple and elegant.

Shakil makes about 12 shades of natural colors from such ingredients as indigo, rust iron, haldi (turmeric), pomegranate skin, madder root and alizarine, cutch (*Acacia catechu*), henna, tea leaves, onion skins, and more. And the huge library of wood-block patterns his father, Kasam, created over the last three decades are helping Shakil to create a beautiful visual language. And to ensure a perfect sense of harmony, he uses high-quality handmade textiles for the natural-dye batiks.

In the last three years, a steady flow of travelers have come to Shakil's remote workshop in Mundra, people who hope to experience a personal narrative in textiles that have withstood

the cyclical nature of the consumer market. "People respond to authenticity instinctively. When someone visits our workshop, we begin with our batik collection of scarves that use azo-free synthetic dyes. People like them and appreciate them; they respond to the craftsmanship and the technique. But as we move on to natural-dyed batik textiles, the entire atmosphere in the room changes. There is fresh new energy. Everyone becomes more awake. People get more engaged with the textiles. They hold them close to their skin. Smell them. Questions about the craft, the history, the process, the natural dyes begin to flow along with the textiles. Until the chai comes to the table. Then we all take a small break, sipping chai with smiles on our faces."

kitchen confidential

Linda Ligon

I SOMETIMES DEFY THE SENSIBLE RULES laid out in this publication and all the other ones on natural dyeing that you might have read. I occasionally dye things in my kitchen in my daily pots and pans with no rubber gloves or dust masks or precision scales. In other words, I sometimes dye things as if I were making soup.

I have one rock-solid rule I never break when following this renegade path, though: I don't use anything I wouldn't put in my mouth or feed to my family. I thought it would be fun to dye some jersey loops and make myself some new hot pads, using only things I could find in my kitchen. Here's what I found:

- Green tea = tannin
- Food-grade pickling alum = mordant (*Well, I wouldn't put this in my mouth or my tongue would shrivel. But I use it for my dill pickles, no problem.*)
- Yellow onion skins = rust-colored dye
- Red onion skins = dark gray-green dye
- Saffron, just a pinch = bright yellow dye

I could have found more: coffee and tea for tans, red cabbage for gray-blue (but it would have faded quickly), beets for rosy pink (also would have faded quickly), and so on. If you're using leftovers from the vegetable crisper or peelings from the compost, then you're not out much if it doesn't work.

But first things first. White cotton jersey loops aren't so easy to come by. I found one source (see page 109), and they are great quality, all the same size, no scouring necessary. They have a little bit of some fiber to give them stretch, but otherwise, they are all cotton and perfect for my little potholder loom.

Following the procedures in Catharine Ellis's excellent guidance on mordants (pages 66–75), I first applied tannin to my loops. This process consisted of four or five teabags simmered in a couple of quarts of water, cooled, with the loops left to steep therein for a couple of hours.

Green tea, pickling alum, onion skins, and a dab of saffron result in cheerful, almost edible colors on cotton jersey loops.

grocery-store carrots don't seem to have much color in them. I just got a pale ick. So I sacrificed a half teaspoon of precious saffron. It doesn't take much to get a vivid monk's-robe gold. The onion skins, of which I used a few handfuls, especially the red ones, are always a surprise. If I had used fewer, my loops would have been more green-gray than gray-green. In every case, I used my old 2½-quart stainless steel pan filled two-thirds with water. I strained out the dyestuff after an hour or so of low simmering, then immersed the loops. (It's important to keep the loops below simmering or they will lose their elasticity.) I left them in there for quite a while, even overnight in some cases. You see my results.

If you don't know how to make a jersey loop hot pad, and don't have a friend sufficiently aged enough to teach you, get a copy of *Potholder Loom Designs: 140 Colorful Patterns.* You probably won't need all 140, but it's nice to have so many choices.

So in parting, let me reiterate: In making my hot pad, I have broken many important rules, such as:

- Never use your cooking pots for dyeing.
- Work in a well-ventilated area; use an outdoor heat source if possible.
- Always wear a dust mask and rubber gloves.
- Measure with precision and keep careful notes.

I respect and honor these rules and strongly recommend them. But sometimes it's okay to relax and just have fun, so long as you're careful to follow my one rock-solid rule (above).

How red onion skins give gray-green dye is one of nature's (or plant chemistry's) mysteries.

Then I mordanted them. Now, admittedly, aluminum acetate would have yielded brighter, maybe longer-lasting colors, but it would also have called for that dust mask and separate pots and so forth. Plus I didn't have any in my cupboard. So I settled for old-fashioned pickling alum: a scant handful (maybe 3 tablespoons) in a couple of quarts of water, simmered to dissolve, then cooled. I soaked my tannin-rich loops in it for an hour or two, keeping the temperature well below simmering.

Then came the fun: simmering groceries to make richly colored dyebaths. I had intended to use carrot tops for bright yellow, but today's

BOOKS

These titles represent just a small slice of the available literature on natural dyeing. Starred entries were cited by several authors of *Nature's Colorways.*

*Balfour Paul, Jenny. *Indigo: Egyptian Mummies to Blue Jeans.* Rev. ed. London: British Museum Press, 2011.

*Boutrup, Joy, and Catharine Ellis. *The Art and Science of Natural Dyes.* Atglen, Pennsylvania: Schiffer Publishing, 2019.

Bryan, Nonabah G. *Navajo Native Dyes: Their Preparation and Use.* US Bureau of Indian Affairs, 1940.

*Cardon, Dominique. *Natural Dyes: Sources, Tradition, Technology and Science.* London: Archetype Publications, 2007.

*Dean, Jenny, and Karen Diadick Casselman. *Wild Color: The Complete Guide to Making and Using Natural Dyes.* Rev. ed. New York: Potter Craft, 2010.

Duerr, Sasha. *Natural Palettes: Inspiration from Plant-Based Color.* Hudson, New York: Princeton Architectural Press, 2020.

Flint, India. *Eco Colour: Botanical Dyes for Beautiful Textiles.* Millers Point, New South Wales, Australia: Murdoch Books, 2008; Loveland, Colorado: Interweave Press, 2008.

Harrisville Designs and Rachel Snack. *Potholder Loom Designs: 140 Colorful Patterns.* Atglen, Pennsylvania: Schiffer Publishing, 2019.

*Liles, J. N. *The Art and Craft of Natural Dyeing: Traditional Recipes for Modern Use.* Knoxville, Tennessee: University of Tennessee Press, 1990.

Marshall, John. *Singing the Blues with John Marshall as Your Guide: Soulful Dyeing for All Eternity.* Covelo, California: St. Titus Press, 2018.

Purvis, William. *Lichens.* London: Natural History Museum, 2000; Washington, DC: Smithsonian Books, 2000.

Recker, Keith. *True Colors: World Masters of Natural Dye and Pigments.* Rev. ed. Loveland, Colorado: Thrums Books, 2020.

Vejar, Kristine, and Adrienne Rodriguez. *Journeys in Natural Dyeing: Techniques for Creating Color at Home.* New York: Abrams, 2020.

JOURNAL ARTICLES

Cardon, Dominique, Iris Brémaud, Anita Quye, and Jenny Balfour Paul. "Exploring Color from the Past: In the Steps of Eighteenth-Century Dyers from France and England." *Textile Museum Journal,* Volume 47, 2020.

Haar, Sherry J. "Eco Prints: Dyeing and Printing with Plants: Sustainable Practices for Color Effects." Paper presented at the 2011 Sustainability Conference, Educating for Sustainability, Kansas State University, Manhattan, Kansas.

Quye, Anita, Dominique Cardon, and Jenny Balfour Paul. "The Crutchley Archive: Red Colours on Wool Fabrics from Master Dyers, London 1716–1744." *Textile History,* Volume 51, issue 2, 2020.

GOODS

Botanical Colors, botanicalcolors.com. Natural-dye extracts, supplies, and blog.

Cotton Clouds, cottonclouds.com. White cotton jersey loops, available in 12-ounce, 5- and 10- pound bags.

Cultural Cloth, culturalcloth.com. Online or on-site sales of natural-dyed, block-printed, and batik fabrics from India and elsewhere.

Dharma Trading Company, dharmatrading.com. All things dyeing.

Earthues, earthues.com. Natural-dye extracts and other supplies.

Maiwa, maiwa.com. Extensive selection of naturaldye supplies, dyeing information, events.

Rowland and Chinami Ricketts, rickettsindigo.com. A highly recommended source for seed of Japanese indigo (*Persicaria tinctorium*). Get on the mailing list in fall for information on growing and ordering information.

ONLINE RESOURCES AND COMMUNITY WEBSITES

Too many to list! These are pertinent to articles in this issue, or have been recommended by our authors.

Growing a Dye Garden, growingadyegarden.wordpress.com. Blog of projects at the Janice Ford Memorial Dye Garden at Chatfield Farms.

Mycopigments, mycopigments.com. Website of Alissa Allen, mushroom and lichen dyer; includes information on events.

Printing with Botanicals, Facebook group sharing processes and results with beautiful photography.

The Dogwood Dyer, thedogwooddyer.com. Website and beautifully photographed blog of Liz Spencer, dyer and gardener.

The Maiwa Guide to Natural Dyes, naturaldyes.ca.

The Plant Mordant Project, plantmordant.org. Details the use of symplocos, a plant-based mordant.

Natural Dyeing and Botanical Printing Safety Precautions, courtesy of Wendy Feldberg

- **Use dedicated equipment** (including pots, spoons, and other tools) for dyeing and ecoprinting; do not use any dyeing equipment for food preparation.
- **Wear a mask** when using powdered mordants and dyes, as fine particles are easily inhaled.
- **Wear gloves** when handling iron liquid and rusted metals.
- **Wear gloves** when handling plants if you know your skin is generally sensitive.
- **When heat-processing plants, work outside whenever possible;** inside, ensure good ventilation.
- **Do not use plants known to be toxic,** even if older dye manuals might recommend them (such as lily of the valley).
- **Choose alum** (alum acetate for cellulose fibers, potassium alum sulfate for protein fibers) **and/or iron as mordants** for ecoprints.
- **Use metallic copper** such as a dyepot or bundling rod for ecoprints; avoid using copper acetate as modifier.
- **Dispose of alum and ferrous sulfate mordants in the garden.** Dilute the liquid with water; do not pour near garden ponds or where it could pool. Compost spent dyeplants.
- **Allow the vinegar in ferrous acetate to evaporate outdoors;** use the orange sediment as pigment.

coming together

ONCE UPON A TIME there were natural-dye workshops and conferences. Small ones, large ones, local, national, international. Waiting for those to return, we've spent the past few months creating our version of a stellar natural-dye gathering—on paper. Teachers, artists, researchers, and gardeners, they've given their all to make natural color come alive in these pages.

Consider the Crutchley Sisters (or Coven, or Posse, depending on whom you ask). **Anita Quye** is a senior lecturer and Professor of Textile Conservation at the University of Glasgow. **Dominique Cardon** is Directrice de Recherche Emérite, CNRS Laboratoire d'Histoire et d'Archéologie, Lyon, France. She has delved into dyeing in Ireland, Peru, Egypt, China—and beyond. **Jenny Balfour Paul,** Honorary Senior Research Fellow at Exeter University, is a writer, artist, dyer, traveler, curator, and international lecturer—wherever there is indigo, there she is. Now imagine these three women shut up in a room together over a couple of years with a hoard of 280-year-old dye samples and recipes. What's emerging is a rich body of work that vividly brings to life the world of eighteenth-century London and one of the families that created its glorious palettes.

We've swooned over **John Marshall**'s precise, lovely paste-resist natural-dyed textiles for years, and we've seen him teach the exacting, traditional Japanese techniques for creating them. What he's done for *Nature's Colorways,* though, is proof of his generosity and scope as a teacher. He has taken the chemistry of indigo back to the basics, the cellular level, in easy-to-follow language and concepts. Then he's shown how to use this knowledge to achieve heavenly blues and blue-greens with minimal time and effort. And he makes it fun! We thank his student Liz Spencer (thedogwooddyer .com) for sharing photos taken during and after one of John's workshops at his studio near Mendocino, California.

Thinking about botanical printing, we found ourselves torn between approaches: Artistic or crafty? Accessible or rigorous? How-to or try-anything? **Wendy Feldberg** looked at our list and said, "Yes, please!" Wendy's generous approach to sharing her practices and knowledge make her blog, *Threadborne,* a rich resource for artists and dyers. With her stunning Ontario garden tucked in for the winter, Wendy measured and formulated her article with as much care and creativity as the inks she makes from her favorite natural-dye materials.

When we were in Guatemala a few years ago, we found we were following in the footsteps of **Donna Brown**—she had been working just days before with her colleague Catharine Ellis to teach a group of Maya women in San Rafael, Alta Verapaz, how to use natural dyes. Her mission in helping establish the Chatfield Farm dye garden in Denver, which she describes on page 46, is all about teaching, too—school kids, the general public, whoever passes through. Teaching natural dyeing has been Donna's focus for more than 30 years.

Lichens are right down there with slime molds as some of the most overlooked but intriguing members of the natural world. **Alissa Allen** knows her lichens, and better yet, she knows how to coax an unlikely array of color from them. She's been collecting, learning, experimenting, and teaching lichen and mushroom dyeing for more than 15 years. It's not just about color, though—Alissa is passionate about the critical role of these odd players in the greater ecosystem. She's most at home in the great outdoors of the Pacific Northwest.

Catharine Ellis has come full circle since learning about natural dyeing in the Navajo Nation in the 1970s, where alum was something you picked up off the ground or dug from a stream bank. Mastering chemical dyeing came next, and developing the concept of loom-woven shibori patterning, both of which she taught for years at Haywood Community College in North Carolina. Moving to a rural home on retirement, she realized that chemical dyeing wouldn't be compatible with her well and septic system, so she returned to natural dyeing. Her dye garden provides a spectrum of vivid colors, and her partnership with master dyer Joy Boutrup has resulted in an important book on mordants (see "For Further Exploration," page 109).

Artist **Kenya Miles** loves natural dyes so much that she named her son Indigo. As artist-in-residence at the Maryland Institute College of Art, farmer at the Parks and People Foundation, and founder of the dye project Blue Light Junction, Kenya is cultivating the natural-color possibilities of urban Baltimore. Stepping away from the dye garden to write about tannin, iron, and mud dye might seem strangely monochrome, but

the colorful history and traditions of this worldwide tradition are right up her alley.

If people still had Rolodexes, **Keith Recker**'s would take a prize for heft. His network in the global world of artisan crafts is wide and deep, so when we asked if he knew people working with iron and tannin, he immediately began ticking off the possibilities. Keith's work with the Hand/Eye Foundation and magazine (which he founded), the International Folk Art Market, and Aid to Artisans in its early years have helped him build these connections—in his spare time. His "day jobs" currently include being co-owner and editor-in-chief of *TABLE* magazine as well as consulting in the international world of color.

When we asked **Mary Anne Wise** if she knew any artisans in India who were working with natural dyes, the answer was a foregone conclusion. Of course she did! Mary Anne and her business partner, Jody Slocum, have traveled the world collecting artisanal textiles for Cultural Cloth, an online and walk-in store in Maiden Rock, Wisconsin. They don't just buy textiles for resale, though—they create relationships with the artisans, visiting their homes and workshops and studios and experiencing firsthand the human connections inherent in the cloth.

As she was developing her article on Sufiyan Khatri, Mary Anne reached out to her friend **Satish Reddy,** who had another textile story to tell, that of his friend Shakil Khatri. Satish left a career in IT to follow his passion for the folk arts of India. His pursuit led him to Bhuj, Gujarat, where he applies his technical savvy and language skills to promote many of the talented artists in the Kutch.

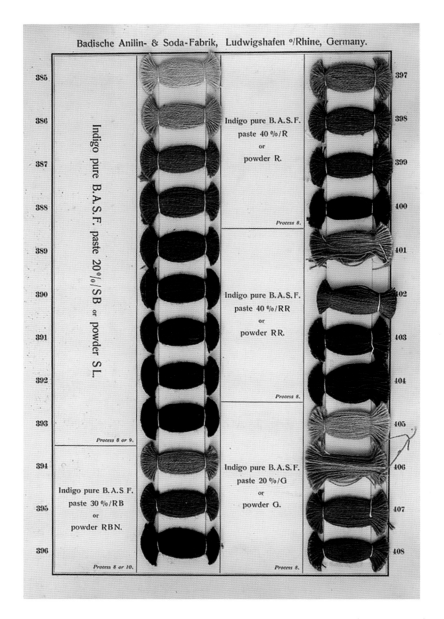

Badische Anilin- & Soda-Fabrik, Ludwigshafen o/Rhine, Germany.

an end and a beginning

IN 1878, German chemist Adolf von Baeyer discovered a way to create synthetic indigo. His discovery led to commercial production in 1897, and to a Nobel Peace Prize in 1905. What you see here is a sample page from a 1900 sales book of BASF (Badische Anilin- und Soda-Fabrik), sole importer to the United States in those early years of pure synthetic indigo, with recipes suitable for 234-gallon vats. Recipes for its use include zinc dust, slaked lime, caustic soda, and hydrosulfite concentrate, and sometimes a chrome mordant. Synthetic indigo has been an industrial juggernaut for more than a century, yet people still are drawn to the authenticity and inherent beauty of plant-derived indigo. The magic lives on.